SIMPLY

SABRINA GHAYOUR

Darling Mathew—my brother, chief taster, wise teacher, and much more—food always tastes so much better with you at our table.

SIMPLY
SABRINA GHAYOUR

EASY EVERYDAY DISHES
FROM THE BESTSELLING AUTHOR OF
Persiana

MITCHELL BEAZLEY

An Hachette UK Company
www.hachette.co.uk

First published in Great Britain in 2020 by Mitchell Beazley,
an imprint of Octopus Publishing Group Ltd
Carmelite House
50 Victoria Embankment
London EC4Y 0DZ
www.octopusbooks.co.uk

Distributed in the US by Hachette Book Group
1290 Avenue of the Americas
4th and 5th Floors, New York, NY 10104

Distributed in Canada by Canadian Manda Group
664 Annette St., Toronto, Ontario, Canada M6S 2C8

ISBN 978 1 78472 703 1

A CIP catalog record for this book is available from
the British Library.

Printed and bound in China

10 9 8 7 6 5 4 3 2 1

Publishing Director: Stephanie Jackson
Senior Managing Editor: Sybella Stephens
Copy Editor: Jo Richardson
Senior Designer: Jaz Bahra
Photographer: Kris Kirkham
Food Stylist: Laura Field
Props Stylist: Agathe Gits
Senior Production Manager: Peter Hunt

Publisher's notes
Vegetarians should look for the "V" symbol on cheese to
ensure it is made with vegetarian rennet. Eggs should be
medium unless otherwise stated. The FDA advises that
certain people, including children, older adults, pregnant
women, and people with weakened immune systems (such
as transplant recipients and individuals with HIV/AIDS, cancer,
or diabetes) should avoid consuming raw or lightly cooked eggs,
and should use pasteurized eggs/egg products when preparing
recipes that call for raw or undercooked eggs. Once prepared,
refrigerate and use promptly.

Contents

Introduction

Being an only child whose parents didn't cook meant that I grew up unafraid to experiment, to break rules, to deviate from tradition, and, at times, to fail miserably and start over. It was quite a galvanizing experience because, as you grow up, you cook without seeing obstacles or limitations and follow your gut and palate instincts about what feels good. More often than not it ends up tasting good, too.

I look back at all that I've learned in my food career and I realize that, perhaps as with you, I have evolved and improved in technique. I've gained more confidence in what may once have been obscure to me, and am now so comfortable in my simple approach that, while I'll always be firmly rooted in the flavors of Iran and the Middle East, it's impossible to stick a specific label on my approach. It's just…Simply Sabrina.

As well as becoming at ease with blending together flavors of my heritage and those of my Western upbringing, my thirst for knowledge and curiosity about the food and flavors of other regions and cultures of the world have also enriched my cooking. My travels have introduced me to ingredients not typical of the Middle East that I now use to bolster flavor, create depth, and, most importantly, provide satisfaction in every mouthful.

I wish I could tell you I have cultivated some kind of solid structure in the way I research my recipes, but the truth is, I haven't. As I cook, eat, and learn, I simplify, create, and pass on to you, having tested (and tested and tested) each recipe to produce the most simple and effective results. In my normal everyday life, I cook every single day, even on vacation. I usually can't stand to be away from the kitchen for more than a few days, which means I always choose apartments instead of hotels so that I can carry on cooking, tasting, and constantly coming up with new ideas and inspiration to use at home. The majority of what makes the cut in my domestic culinary repertoire and shines as a clear favorite is what eventually makes it into my cookery classes and, in turn, into my books.

This book features a selection of my favorite authentic Persian recipes from my childhood, including some long-forgotten dishes that have been brought back to life by my loved ones asking me to try and recreate them. Translating the ingredients, methods, and "you have to do it this way"-isms into simplified, accessible recipes is the challenging part. Every culture that reveres its culinary traditions will swear that you "must only use this" and you "can't do that." All this tends to do is freak most people out, so much that they only ever attempt to make the recipe once and then cast it aside. I never cooked by those rules because I wasn't taught by anyone and so was never shown the singular way in which something should be done. I have reworked and retested these recipes to deliver the fastest, simplest, and most delicious way to cook them in everyday life without too much stress or a myriad of unnecessary or hard-to-find ingredients.

Over the years, the once-embraced "simplicity" of food and cookery has been somewhat sidelined in favor of complexity, modernity, technique, and process, especially in haute cuisine and fine-dining restaurants. While this is all perfectly valid, I am and shall always remain the consummate home cook, favoring simplicity in ingredients, recipes, and techniques, and yet complexity in flavor and depth of satisfaction. So when it comes to recipe creation, I've always prided myself on trying my very best to make my recipes as straightforward as possible. I keep ingredient lists short and unexotic but without compromising the end result, and only garnishing for the purpose of flavor and not visual appeal. If I can strip out an ingredient and still produce a flavorful dish, I will always strive to omit it to keep matters simple, as well as more budget-friendly.

Over time, I have received a great education from my readers about what they enjoy most about my recipes. This has helped me identify an important framework for them that perhaps wasn't so apparent to me when I first started. So, in this book you will find everyday dishes that are, for the most part, simple, flavorful, and economical, with the occasional special treat thrown in here and there.

As with all my recipes, you can, of course, substitute or omit ingredients to suit your personal tastes. This is my fifth book, so I think you already know this is very much my ethos and that, baking aside, the best recipes usually allow the home cook a little freedom and individuality. When you keep flavors and proceedings simple, you always produce the best results, and generate confidence and enthusiasm for cooking the type of food you love the most.

So here you have simply good ingredients, simply prepared to create simply wonderful flavors. It really is just that simple.

Simply yours,

Sabrina Ghayour

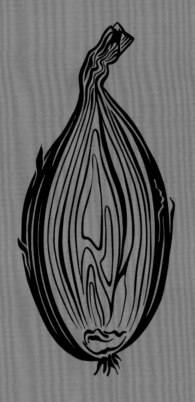

Effortless eating

Thyme & za'atar roasted tomatoes
with strained yogurt balls

Give me a plate of this with a little lightly toasted bread, shut the door, and leave me in peace. I have always loved tomatoes, but a little herb injection and some honey make this humble dish an absolute game changer. It's the kind of dish that you don't want to plate up individually; you simply want to push your bread about the plate to create different textures and flavors and then mop it all up. And who could blame you? For me, that's the best kind of food.

MAKES 16 TO 18

2 cups Greek yogurt

1lb 2oz baby plum tomatoes

1 tablespoon olive oil

2 tablespoons za'atar

4 sprigs of thyme, leaves picked

1 lemon, for grating

2 tablespoons liquid honey

1 teaspoon pul biber chile flakes

sea salt flakes and freshly ground
  black pepper

The day before you want to serve this, mix the yogurt with 2 tablespoons salt and then spoon into a cheesecloth bag. Let strain over a bowl overnight in the refrigerator.

The next day, preheat the oven to 400°F. Line a baking pan with nonstick parchment paper.

Place the tomatoes on the prepared baking pan, add the olive oil, za'atar, thyme leaves, and salt and pepper. Use your hands to mix until the tomatoes are well coated with the oil and seasonings. Roast for 20 minutes until the tomatoes are beginning to char, then remove from the oven and let cool.

Remove the strained yogurt from the cloth bag and shape into balls about 1¼ inch in diameter.

Arrange the cooled roasted tomatoes and yogurt balls on a plate. Grate some lemon zest onto them, drizzle with the honey, and sprinkle with the pul biber before serving.

SIMPLY DELICIOUS WITH...

Green Bean Salad with Tahini, Preserved Lemon & Pine Nuts (see page 47) and Lamb & Mint Kofte (see page 78).

Mozzarella, olive & za'atar pizzettes

I came up with these when I needed to use up some mozzarella and I resorted to raiding my spice rack. It's a marriage of the Lebanese *mana'eesh* (za'atar-rubbed breads) and the humble Italian pizza, but ultimately very different from both of them. These are stupidly simple and surprisingly delicious—my two favorite qualities in a good recipe.

MAKES 4

4 mini tortilla wraps
olive oil, for drizzling
2 heaped teaspoons za'atar
5½oz ball of mozzarella (not buffalo
    mozzarella), torn into ½-inch pieces
12 Kalamata olives, pitted and sliced
2 tomatoes, cut into ½-inch dice
sea salt flakes and freshly ground
    black pepper

Preheat your oven to its highest setting. Line a large baking pan with nonstick parchment paper.

Place the tortilla wraps on the prepared baking pan and drizzle with just enough olive oil so that when you rub it in it coats the whole wrap. Divide the za'atar between the tortillas, reserving a little for seasoning the topping. Then divide the cheese, olives, and tomatoes between them.

Season with salt and pepper and the remaining za'atar, then bake for 4 to 5 minutes until the cheese has melted. Serve immediately.

SIMPLY DELICIOUS WITH...

Green-Yogurt-dressed Baby Romaine Lettuce with Burnt Hazelnuts (see page 44) or Marinated Steak with Labneh, Pul Biber Butter & Crispy Onions (see page 188).

Cauliflower & cumin soup

The first time I tried cauliflower soup, no exaggeration, I was head over heels in love with it. I cannot understand why it isn't more popular. Despite cauliflower's delicate nature when cooked, it can handle bold spices extremely well, and cumin is really one of the best pairings with it. Soups needn't be a humble affair. They can be rich and decadent as well as comforting, and not just an opening act but very much the star of the show. This example, while simple in terms of ingredients, is a warming wonder of a soup.

SERVES 3 TO 4

1 heaped tablespoon cumin seeds, toasted and ground (see Tip)

olive oil

1 large onion, cut into coarse chunks

1 large cauliflower, with outer leaves, cut into coarse chunks

1½ quarts boiling water

¾ cup heavy cream

sea salt flakes and freshly ground black pepper

Heat a large saucepan over medium heat, drizzle in a little olive oil, and add the onion and cauliflower along with the ground cumin. Season well with salt and pepper, stir, then pour in the boiling water. Cover the pan with a lid and let simmer for 20 to 25 minutes, or until the cauliflower is cooked through. Remove from the heat.

Using a hand-held stick blender, blend to a smooth consistency, adding more water if necessary. Pour in the cream and stir well, then check and adjust the seasoning. Return the soup to the heat and warm through, then serve immediately with bread and garnished with a drizzle of olive oil.

SIMPLY DELICIOUS WITH...

Curry-spiced Parmesan Toast (see page 19) or Cilantro & Feta Spiced Loaf (see page 235).

TIP

To toast spices, heat a dry skillet over medium heat and add the spices.
Shake the pan for a minute or so until the spices release their aroma.
Transfer the toasted seeds to a mortar and pestle and grind to a coarse powder.

Spiced carrot & tamarind soup

Carrots make for a wonderful soup but usually with a flavor partner, as on their own their sweetness can be a little overpowering or one-dimensional. Tamarind is a great pairing with the humble carrot, providing it with a rounded acidity that complements but doesn't kill or compete with the vegetable's natural flavor.

SERVES 4 TO 6

olive oil

2 large onions, coarsely chopped

3¼lb carrots, peeled and cut
    into coarse chunks

1 teaspoon ground cinnamon,
    plus extra to garnish (optional)

1 teaspoon ground turmeric

1 teaspoon ground ginger

1 teaspoon paprika

1 tablespoon garlic granules

1 tablespoon unsweetened
    tamarind paste

1½ quarts boiling water

sea salt flakes and freshly ground
    black pepper

Place a large saucepan over medium heat and pour in enough olive oil to coat the bottom of the pan. Add the onions and carrots and cook for a few minutes, without browning. Add the cinnamon, turmeric, ginger, paprika, and garlic granules and stir until the carrots and onions are well coated in the oil and spices. Season with a generous amount of salt and pepper, then add the tamarind paste and measured boiling water and stir well.

Reduce the heat to medium-low and gently simmer the soup for 30 minutes, or until the carrots and onions are cooked through. Remove from the heat.

Using a hand-held stick blender, blitz the soup until smooth. Check and adjust the seasoning, then serve drizzled with olive oil and sprinkled with a little extra cinnamon, if liked.

SIMPLY DELICIOUS WITH...

Cilantro & Feta Spiced Loaf (see page 235).

Curry-spiced Parmesan toasts

I've always been more of a savory than a sweet girl, especially at breakfast time, but usually at lunch and dinner, too. French toast is something I love, but savory French toast really is something else, and this little experiment of mine paid off beautifully. Parmesan has such depth of flavor. Its intense umami-laden complexity means it can be paired with spice and other feisty ingredients so much more than many other cheeses. It's also the perfect cheese for encrusting this spiced toast, which I must warn you is somewhat addictive and not just suited to breakfast, making a rather wonderful, lazy supper, too. I love to serve them with a spicy lime pickle chutney or a sweet mango chutney.

MAKES 4

3 eggs

2 teaspoons curry powder

2 teaspoons garlic granules

1 teaspoon cayenne pepper

3 tablespoons milk

4 slices of sourdough

3½ tablespoons butter

1 cup finely grated Parmesan cheese

sea salt flakes and freshly ground
    black pepper

Put the eggs, curry powder, garlic granules, cayenne, milk, and some salt and pepper into a shallow bowl (or food container) and beat together until evenly combined.

Heat a large skillet over medium heat. Meanwhile, soak the slices of sourdough in the egg mixture, turning them over to ensure both sides absorb the mixture.

Once the bread has absorbed all the egg mixture, add half the butter to the hot pan, and when melted, fry the first 2 bread slices for 3 to 4 minutes on the underside. Meanwhile, sprinkle one-quarter of the Parmesan over the top side of each slice and gently press it into the bread. Then carefully flip the bread slices over and cook for a further 3 to 4 minutes until the cheese is melted and golden. Remove from the pan and keep warm under foil (or eat them!) while you repeat with the remaining ingredients, then serve immediately.

SIMPLY DELICIOUS WITH...

Cauliflower & Cumin Soup (see page 15) or Spiced Carrot & Tamarind Soup (see page 16).

Date & ginger chicken wings

Chicken wings will always be one of my all-time favorite things to eat. They're easy on the pocket and great finger food, too. I am always coming up with new and interesting sauces, marinades, and ways to cook them. This is quite a different creation from anything I've ever tasted before, but the one thing I know is that sticky and spicy always make a great flavor combination when it comes to wings, and these don't disappoint. Don't be afraid to let them get nice and deeply charred in the oven—it simply adds to the flavor.

SERVES 4 TO 6

2¼lb chicken wings

FOR THE MARINADE

9oz large dates, pitted and coarsely
    chopped
2- to 2¾-inch piece of fresh ginger
    root, peeled and coarsely chopped
2 tablespoons rice vinegar

2 tablespoons garlic oil
1 heaped tablespoon ground ginger
1 tablespoon garlic granules
3 tablespoons boiling water
2 heaped tablespoons Greek yogurt
juice of 1 lemon
sea salt flakes

Put all the ingredients for the marinade into a food processor along with a generous amount of salt, and blitz until smooth.

Place the chicken wings in a nonmetallic bowl or other container, pour in the marinade, then use your hands to work it into the chicken until well coated. Cover the bowl or container with plastic wrap and place in the refrigerator to marinate for 1 hour, or overnight if liked.

Preheat the oven to 425°F. Line your largest baking pan with nonstick parchment paper.

Arrange the chicken wings on the prepared baking pan and roast for 45 minutes, turning them over halfway through the cooking time, until dark brown, charred on top, and cooked through. Serve immediately.

SIMPLY DELICIOUS WITH...

Baked Sweet Potato Fries with Za'atar & Garlic (see page 34) and Tomato & Peanut Salad with Tamarind, Ginger & Honey Dressing (see page 137).

Green chicken

This is what happens when you have a lot of herbs to use up and want to make the quickest roast chicken for supper. Green chicken has become a bit of a thing in our house, and the herb content has varied wildly, but I have now found a balance I'm happy with. These chunks of aromatic, tender chicken are delicious served in wraps, but they also make a great addition to salads of every description.

SERVES 4 TO 6

1½lb boneless, skinless chicken breasts, cut into 1½-inch chunks

FOR THE MARINADE
1 small pack (about 1oz) of fresh cilantro, coarsely chopped
1 small pack (about 1oz) of flat leaf parsley, coarsely chopped
1 small pack (about 1oz) of chives, coarsely snipped
2 tablespoons dried dill weed
1 tablespoon ground fenugreek
1 tablespoon garlic granules

½ teaspoon chile flakes
¼ cup Greek yogurt, plus extra to serve
1 tablespoon olive oil
sea salt flakes and freshly ground black pepper

TO SERVE
tortilla wraps
tomatoes
sliced red onion
cilantro leaves
pul biber chile flakes

Put all the ingredients for the marinade into a food processor and blitz until you have a smooth puree.

Place the chicken chunks in a mixing bowl, pour in the marinade, and mix together well. Cover the bowl with plastic wrap and place in the refrigerator to marinate overnight. Alternatively, you can bake the chicken as soon as your oven is up to temperature.

Preheat your oven to its highest setting. Line a large baking pan with nonstick parchment paper.

Spread the chicken out on the prepared baking pan and bake for about 12 minutes until cooked through. Serve immediately in tortilla wraps with more yogurt, tomatoes, sliced red onion, cilantro leaves, and pul biber.

SIMPLY DELICIOUS WITH...
Baked Sweet Potato Fries with Za'atar & Garlic (see page 34).

Turmeric chicken kebabs

Turmeric really is the key ingredient in this fragrant chicken marinade, which is paired with the vibrant citrus zing of lime and the sweet, rounded finish of honey. These kebabs can be cooked either on the stove, in the oven, or on a barbecue (see Tip), and they are so versatile they can be served with wraps, rice, fries, or even just on their own.

SERVES 4 TO 6

4 boneless, skinless chicken breasts
    (about 1½lb total weight)
sweet chilli sauce, to serve

FOR THE MARINADE
2-inch piece of fresh turmeric,
    scrubbed and finely grated
1 tablespoon garlic granules

finely grated zest and juice of
    1 lime
2 tablespoons plain yogurt
1 generous tablespoon liquid honey
1 tablespoon olive oil
sea salt flakes and freshly ground
    black pepper

Put all the ingredients for the marinade into a plastic food container and mix together.

Cut each chicken breast lengthwise into 3 equal long strips. Add to the marinade in the food container and seal securely with the lid. Shake well to coat the chicken in the marinade. Place in the refrigerator to marinate for 30 minutes to 1 hour, or overnight if liked.

Thread each strip of marinated chicken onto small wooden or metal skewers. Cook in a ridged grill pan over high heat for 3 to 4 minutes on each side or until nicely browned and cooked through.

Alternatively, preheat your oven to its highest setting. Line a large baking pan with nonstick parchment paper. Lay the kebabs on the prepared baking pan and bake for 10 to 12 minutes or until cooked through. Serve immediately with sweet chilli sauce.

SIMPLY DELICIOUS WITH...
Corn, Black Bean & Avocado Salad (see page 139) or Polow-e-Bademjan-o-Felfel (see page 125).

TIP
You can also cook these kebabs on the barbecue. If using wooden skewers, soak them in water for 30 minutes before using. Cook over medium-low heat for about 5 to 6 minutes on each side until nicely browned and cooked through.

Pomegranate shallots

Roasted shallots have always been one of my favorite accompaniments to roasted meats. There is something about their sweet, soft flesh that I love mashing up and mixing with every bite of my meal (I could eat a whole tray of them, to be honest). This version is slightly different, as the pomegranate molasses adds quite a tart flavor to contrast with the natural sweetness of the shallots. I would suggest making a double quantity if there are more than two of you, as it's really worth it and involves little extra effort. The final flourish of sumac gives the dish a pronounced citric bite, just as the pomegranate molasses has intensified and sweetened it.

SERVES 2 TO 4

3 tablespoons pomegranate molasses

1 generous tablespoon liquid honey

1 teaspoon ground cinnamon

14oz long shallots, peeled but kept whole

1 teaspoon sumac

sea salt flakes and freshly ground
    black pepper

Preheat the oven to 350°F.

Select an ovenproof dish that just about accommodates the shallots with no room to spare (this is because you need the liquid to almost cover the shallots as they roast).

In a small bowl, mix together the pomegranate molasses, honey, cinnamon, and a generous amount of salt and pepper until evenly combined.

Lay the shallots in the ovenproof dish and pour the sauce over them. Don't worry that the sauce won't cling to the shallots at this uncooked stage.

Roast the shallots for 1 hour 20 minutes, basting them in the sauce every 20 minutes. Sprinkle the sumac on top for the final 20 minutes of cooking, at the end of which the shallots should be tender and easily pierced with a sharp knife. Remove from the oven and serve immediately.

SIMPLY DELICIOUS WITH...

Spice-rubbed Spatchcocked Squab (see page 55) or Pot-roasted Brisket with Harissa & Spices (see page 59).

Charred zucchini
with lemon, oregano & pul biber

This is one of my regular, quick summer vegetable dishes. It's an absolute lazy staple in my house. I encourage you wholeheartedly to char the zucchini nicely because it makes them so irresistible and delicious. I love using this oven method—high temperature, short cooking time—which gives such a pleasing result for so many different ingredients, from zucchini and bell peppers to chicken and salmon. The lemon juice brings a wonderful finish to the spicy, charred zucchini. You can enjoy them hot or cold and even add a little feta to serve.

SERVES 4 TO 6

4 zucchini
olive or garlic oil, for drizzling
finely grated zest of 1 lemon
    and juice of ½
2 tablespoons dried wild oregano
1 teaspoon pul biber chile flakes
sea salt flakes and freshly ground
    black pepper

Preheat your oven to its highest setting. Line your largest baking pan with nonstick parchment paper.

Cut the zucchini diagonally into slices ½ inch thick and spread them out on the prepared baking pan. Drizzle generously with olive or garlic oil and sprinkle with all the remaining ingredients, except the lemon juice. Season generously with salt and pepper and then rub the seasonings into and all over the zucchini slices.

Roast the zucchini for 8 minutes, then remove from the oven, squeeze the lemon juice evenly over the zucchini, and roast for a further 6 minutes before serving.

SIMPLY DELICIOUS WITH...

Turmeric Chicken Kebabs (see page 24) or Sea Bream with Spiced Green Olive & Shallot Butter (see page 64).

Mashed cannellini beans
with preserved lemon & tahini

I have a lot of love for the humble bean as found in every guise—salads, stews, soups, dips, and patties. While versatile and flavorsome, they often need an additional gentle flavor pairing to bring out their best. Here, I've turned to much bolder flavors, which nevertheless work quite subtly with the cannellini beans. But every now and again you get the most wonderful sharp spike of preserved lemon, which complements their creamy, sweet nature so well.

SERVES 4 TO 6

1lb 2oz dried cannellini beans

3 tablespoons olive oil, plus extra
    for drizzling

2 heaped tablespoons tahini

3 garlic cloves, minced

4 to 5 tablespoons warm water,
    or more if needed

6 preserved lemons, seeded and
    finely chopped

1 small pack (about 1oz) of flat leaf
    parsley, leaves and stalks finely
    chopped

sea salt flakes, if needed, and freshly
    ground black pepper

Soak the cannellini beans in cold water overnight, or for 8 to 10 hours, then drain.

Cook the beans in a saucepan of boiling water for 1½ hours or until cooked, topping off the water as necessary.

Drain the cooked beans and return them to the pan. Add the olive oil, tahini, and garlic and mash the beans coarsely over gentle heat until mashed to your preferred texture.

Pour in the warm water (add more if you prefer a looser consistency), season well with pepper, and mix in the preserved lemons and parsley. Check the seasoning and add a tiny bit of salt if needed, bearing in mind that preserved lemons are in themselves a little salty. Serve immediately drizzled with extra olive oil.

SIMPLY DELICIOUS WITH...

Pot-roasted Brisket with Harissa & Spices (see page 59) or Sea Bream with Spiced Green Olive & Shallot Butter (see page 64).

Slow-cooked lima beans
with oregano, tomatoes & garlic

I am a recent convert to dried beans, and sometimes they really are worth the extra time. I like a little bite in my beans, which canned beans lack, so this garlicky, sauce-laden baked delight is one example of your extra time being well spent. It's hearty but not heavy, rich but only in a really good way, and ideal for sharing.

SERVES 4 TO 6

1¾ cups dried lima beans

9oz baby plum tomatoes, halved

4 to 6 garlic cloves, peeled and bashed but kept whole

generous handful of fresh oregano, coarsely chopped

1 heaped tablespoon tomato puree

2 teaspoons dried oregano

1 teaspoon chile flakes

3½ tablespoons butter

¼ cup olive oil

about 3 cups cold water

generous amount of sea salt flakes and freshly ground black pepper

crusty bread, to serve (optional)

Soak the lima beans in cold water overnight, or for 8 to 10 hours, then drain.

Preheat the oven to 350°F.

Select a rectangular ovenproof dish, about 13 x 10 inches. Add all the ingredients, except the water, to the dish and mix together well, then pour over the measured cold water, or enough to ensure the beans are immersed.

Bake for 2 hours until the beans are completely soft, checking after 1½ hours and topping off the water if necessary. Serve hot, with crusty bread if liked.

SIMPLY DELICIOUS WITH...

Maast-o-Esfenaj (see page 72) or Beet & Feta Lattice (see page 67).

TIP
If you have any leftovers, lightly mash them the next day for something completely different.

Baked sweet potato fries with za'atar & garlic

I can quite happily sit in front of a mountain of any kind of cooked sweet potato and pile through the entire lot with the greatest of ease. I find its light, digestible nature almost dangerously appealing. These are just that, dangerously appealing, although there is actually little danger here because, as we know, sweet potatoes are good for us and baking them makes them even less sinful. The only danger is that, much like me, you'll nail half the pan before they have even hit the plate. But then again, that's not such a bad thing.

SERVES 4 TO 6

3 tablespoons quick-cook polenta

3 tablespoons za'atar

1 heaped tablespoon garlic granules

4 sweet potatoes, peeled and cut into
    ½-inch thick french fries

3 tablespoons olive oil

sea salt flakes and freshly ground
    black pepper

Preheat the oven to 425°F. Line your largest baking pan with nonstick parchment paper.

Mix the polenta, za'atar, garlic granules, and a generous amount of salt and pepper together in a small bowl.

Place the sweet potato fries on the prepared baking pan, drizzle with the olive oil, and use your hands to mix until the fries are well coated in the oil. Sprinkle with the polenta and seasoning mixture and toss to coat the fries evenly.

Spread the fries out on the baking pan and bake for about 30 minutes until soft in the middle and the edges start to brown. Serve immediately.

SIMPLY DELICIOUS WITH...

Turmeric Chicken Kebabs (see page 24) or Crispy Cod Wraps with Salsa & Harissa Lime Mayo (see page 160).

Spiced turmeric mashed potatoes
with cilantro

I've always loved mashed potatoes, but this is the next level taste-wise. It's so comforting, and I'm not sure how it could be improved. I am mad about turmeric and it's no secret that I love chiles, and the natural sweetness of the potatoes means they can handle the spices and chile heat easily. This is a dish I can't recommend enough, even if you are simply looking for an alternative to your usual mashed potatoes on the side.

SERVES 6 TO 8

4½lb russet potatoes, peeled and
    halved, or quartered if large
1 teaspoon cumin seeds
1 teaspoon black mustard seeds
½ cup butter
1 to 2 teaspoons chile flakes, to taste

¾oz fresh turmeric, scrubbed and
    very finely grated
1 small pack (about 1oz) of fresh
    cilantro, finely chopped
sea salt flakes and freshly ground
    black pepper

Cook the potatoes in a large saucepan of salted boiling water for 15 to 20 minutes, or until cooked through. Drain in a colander and set aside to steam dry.

Place the saucepan over medium heat, add the cumin and mustard seeds, and toast them for a few minutes, shaking the pan until they release their aroma. Add the butter, chile flakes, and turmeric and stir until the butter has melted.

Return the potatoes to the pan and season generously with salt and pepper, then mash with the spiced butter until just combined (I like to keep some chunkiness in the texture). Check and adjust the seasoning, and when you're happy with it, add the cilantro and mix well to serve.

SIMPLY DELICIOUS WITH...

Spice-rubbed Spatchcocked Squab (see page 55) or Yogurt & Spice Roasted Salmon (see page 62).

Tomato & garlic rice

This is my kind of quick and lazy rice—especially when I'm cooking many other dishes at the same time or simply too tired to cook rice the Persian way—and a handy one that uses kitchen-cupboard ingredients to bring it together. It's a full-flavored recipe I find myself turning to time and again, and makes a great accompaniment to roasts and stews.

SERVES 4

1¼ cups basmati rice

1 red onion, halved and very thinly sliced
    into half moons

4 garlic cloves, minced

1 small pack (about 1oz) of flat leaf parsley,
    finely chopped

3½ tablespoons butter

¼ cup tomato paste

1 heaped teaspoon garlic granules

1 teaspoon ground coriander

finely grated zest and juice of 1 fat lime

1¾ cups cold water

sea salt flakes and freshly ground
    black pepper

Put all the ingredients into a saucepan with a lid, season with a generous amount of salt and pepper, and stir together well.

If using a gas stove, place over low heat, but if using an electric/induction stove, place over medium-low heat. Cover the pan with the lid and cook for about 30 minutes, or until the rice on the top is tender and cooked through and all the water has been fully absorbed.

SIMPLY DELICIOUS WITH...

Spiced Pork Stew (see page 185) or Turmeric & Black Pepper Braised Lamb Neck (see page 96).

Scallion salad
with sesame & pul biber

Persians love onions of every description, and we eat scallions and onions raw as accompaniments to our meals. This salad is one that I can quite happily eat on the side of roasted meats, stews, sandwiches, and much more. It just seems to go with so many things, and it's ridiculously easy to make, too.

SERVES 4 TO 6

2 teaspoons sesame seeds

2 tablespoons superfine sugar

2 teaspoons rice vinegar

2 teaspoons sesame oil

2 teaspoons pul biber chile flakes

2 bunches of scallions, thinly sliced
    diagonally from root to tip

sea salt flakes and freshly ground black pepper

Put the sesame seeds, sugar, rice vinegar, and sesame oil into a large mixing bowl. Stir well until the sugar dissolves. Stir in the pul biber.

Add the scallions and toss to coat in the dressing.

Season well with salt and pepper, toss again, and serve.

SIMPLY DELICIOUS WITH...

Yogurt & Spice Roasted Salmon (see page 62).

Flame-roasted bell pepper, pistachio & dill weed yogurt

We Eastern types are slightly obsessed with yogurt. It's a staple of the table, whether served plain or combined with cucumber, spinach, or beets, and an essential for any serious meal in an Eastern household. While roasted bell peppers don't feature heavily in Persian cuisine, I very much love the texture, and they always remind me of sun-soaked destinations like Turkey or Greece. The added crunch from the pistachios makes this less of a dip and more of a dish in itself. Lightly toast or chargrill some of your favorite bread and use it as a vessel to scoop this up.

SERVES 4 TO 6

1lb jar (6oz drained weight) red or mixed-colored flame-roasted bell peppers, drained and patted dry

1 long shallot, minced

1 garlic clove, minced

2 cups Greek yogurt

1 small pack (about 1oz) of dill weed, very finely chopped

⅓ cup pistachio slivers (or very coarsely chopped whole nuts)

olive oil, for drizzling

sea salt flakes and freshly ground black pepper

Thinly slice the bell peppers widthwise into ribbons. Put them into a mixing bowl along with the shallot and garlic and give them a stir.

Add the yogurt, dill weed, pistachios, some salt, and a generous amount of pepper, then drizzle with about 1 tablespoon olive oil and stir to combine. Let stand for about 5 minutes and then check and adjust the seasoning to taste.

Spread the yogurt mixture onto a large plate, add a little extra drizzle of olive oil, and a grinding of pepper and serve.

SIMPLY DELICIOUS WITH...

Pomegranate Molasses & Honey-glazed Meatballs (see page 56) or Albaloo Polow (see page 89).

Green-yogurt-dressed Baby Romaine lettuce *with burnt hazelnuts*

If I'm going to eat salad, it has to have lots of flavor, texture, and substance to it in order to win me over. This one is deceptively simple, and I can quite easily demolish half of it in a matter of minutes. The darkly toasted hazelnuts really add something wonderful to it, but the fresh herb-packed dressing is what makes it so good. To make it more of a meal, you can crumble a little feta on top or add cooked chicken if liked.

SERVES 6 TO 8

⅓ cup blanched hazelnuts

4 heads of Baby Romaine lettuce, quartered

2 to 3 small preserved lemons, seeded and finely chopped

sea salt flakes and freshly ground black pepper

FOR THE DRESSING

½ small pack (about ½oz) of dill weed

½ small pack (about ½oz) of flat leaf parsley

½ small pack (about ½oz) of basil

¼ cup Greek yogurt

1 tablespoon olive oil

1 to 2 tablespoons cold water (depending how thick your yogurt is), optional

Preheat the oven to 425°F.

Spread the hazelnuts out on a baking pan and toast in the oven for 6 to 7 minutes until darkly toasted. Remove from the oven and let cool.

Put all the ingredients for the dressing, except the water, into a blender. Season with salt and pepper and blitz until smooth and vibrant green. Add the measured cold water as needed to thin the dressing slightly to a pourable consistency.

Arrange the lettuce quarters on a platter and drizzle with the dressing, then scatter with the chopped preserved lemons. Season well with pepper, top with the toasted hazelnuts, and serve immediately.

SIMPLY DELICIOUS WITH...

Beet & Feta Lattice (see page 67) or Green Bean & Black-eyed Pea Baklava with Feta & Honey (see page 193).

Green bean salad
with tahini, preserved lemon & pine nuts

Green beans are so versatile. I use them in stir-fries, stews, rice, soups, and especially in salads, as they are a great carrier of flavors and dressings. Tahini can be a marvelous ingredient, but it does need other additions to really make it shine, and usually a hit of lemon does the trick beautifully. This wonderful green bean salad is spiked with tangy, salty preserved lemon slices and given a crunch of pine nuts to create the ideal side dish, as well as the perfect lunchbox option to take to work the next day.

SERVES 4

14oz fine green beans
2 preserved lemons
1 fat garlic clove, minced
generous squeeze of lemon juice
1 tablespoon tahini
3 tablespoons warm water
handful of pine nuts
freshly ground black pepper

Cook the green beans in a saucepan of boiling water for about 10 to 12 minutes. The timing will vary depending on their variety and thickness. Drain and rinse under cold running water until cool, then drain well and dry on paper towels.

Cut the preserved lemons in half and thinly slice them into half moons. Set aside.

Put the garlic into a small bowl with the lemon juice. Add the tahini and then mix in the warm water to loosen the mixture (don't use cold water, or the mixture will seize).

Place the green beans in a mixing bowl and pour the dressing over them. Add the preserved lemon slices and season with a generous amount of pepper, then transfer to a plate and scatter with the pine nuts before serving.

SIMPLY DELICIOUS WITH...

Ultimate Falafels (see page 81) or Harissa Chicken Noodle Lettuce Cups (see page 115).

Cucumber, green apple & nigella salad *with feta & dill weed*

Feta always makes a wonderful addition to a salad but here it acts more as a dressing than an ingredient. The refreshing combination of cooling cucumber and sharp yet sweet apple makes it the perfect side dish for so many different meals. Alternatively, you can chop the apple and cucumber finely and serve a dollop on Belgian endive leaves as a light snack.

SERVES 6 TO 8

3½oz feta cheese

3 tablespoons Greek yogurt

2 teaspoons nigella seeds

2 Granny Smith apples, cored, halved, and sliced into half moons

1 large cucumber, peeled, halved lengthwise, and seeds scooped out, then cut into slices ¼ inch thick

1 small pack (about ½oz) of dill weed, finely chopped

sea salt flakes and freshly ground black pepper

1 scallion, sliced diagonally, to garnish

olive oil, for drizzling

Mash the feta into a paste in a mixing bowl. Add the Greek yogurt, a little salt, and a generous amount of pepper and mix together well.

Add 1½ teaspoons of the nigella seeds, the apples, cucumber, and dill weed, then toss the ingredients in the feta mixture until evenly coated.

Arrange the salad on a serving platter, sprinkle with the remaining nigella seeds, and garnish with the scallion. Drizzle with a little olive oil before serving.

SIMPLY DELICIOUS WITH...

Fragrant Fish Cakes with Preserved Lemon Mayonnaise (see page 152) or Seafood, Coconut & Ginger Spiced Rice (see page 156).

Carrot, pistachio & dill weed salad
with lime & honey dressing

Although I love carrots, I have to confess that I often just peel them and eat them raw on their own or use them as a vehicle for hummus. This is a lovely, yet simple, salad with lots of flavor and a nutty flourish of pistachio, too. Texture is a big thing for me and one of the humble carrot's greatest gifts—in addition to its sweet flavor—is that wonderful, juicy crunch.

SERVES 4 TO 6

1lb 2oz carrots, peeled and shredded in a food processor or coarsely grated

½ small red onion, halved and thinly sliced into half moons

½ cup pistachios, coarsely chopped

1 small pack (about 1oz) of dill weed, finely chopped

2 teaspoons nigella seeds

FOR THE DRESSING

2 tablespoons olive oil

finely grated zest and juice of 1 lime

1 generous tablespoon liquid honey

generous amount of sea salt flakes and freshly ground black pepper

Mix all the dressing ingredients together in a small bowl or a measuring cup.

Place all the salad ingredients in a large mixing bowl. When ready to serve, add the dressing to the salad and use your hands to very gently toss the ingredients until evenly coated. Check and adjust the seasoning to taste. Serve immediately.

SIMPLY DELICIOUS WITH...

Steak Tartines with Tarragon & Paprika Butter (see page 129) or Chicken & Apricot Pastries (see page 169).

TIP
Make sure to add the dressing just before serving to stop the carrots from softening. If you're vegan, you can use agave syrup instead of the honey.

Fennel salad
with spinach, cashew & coriander seed dressing

My love for fennel was a slow-burner, but over time I have learned to wholeheartedly embrace all the ways in which it can be enjoyed. I've already written several fennel recipes and I very much wanted to come up with one that was totally different to the more common ways of preparing it, so this particular combination is like nothing you've ever tried before. The cashew nuts give the dressing a lovely texture so that the fennel is entirely enrobed in a rich, satisfying sauce.

SERVES 4 TO 6

2 large fennel bulbs

FOR THE DRESSING
4½oz baby spinach
¾ cup cashew nuts
3 teaspoons sumac, plus 1 teaspoon
    to garnish
2 teaspoons ground coriander

2 teaspoons coriander seeds, toasted
    (see Tip on page 15)
¼ cup olive oil
2 tablespoons lukewarm water
2 tablespoons red wine vinegar
sea salt flakes and freshly ground
    black pepper

Put all the dressing ingredients, except the 1 teaspoon sumac to garnish, into a food processor and blitz until you have a sauce consistency. Add an extra tablespoon of water to thin it down if necessary.

Trim the fennel bulbs, then quarter and thinly slice them. Put the fennel into a mixing bowl, pour the dressing over it, and toss until each slice of fennel is well coated.

Arrange the fennel salad on a plate, sprinkle with the remaining sumac, and serve.

SIMPLY DELICIOUS WITH...
Chorizo, Goat Cheese & Cumin Borek (see page 148) or Tahchin (see page 87).

Spice-rubbed spatchcocked squab

The joy of squab is that it cooks in half the time of a normal-sized chicken. Spatchcocking reduces the cooking time further still and makes for a wonderful, evenly cooked bird with a lovely crisp skin and juicy, tender meat. If that's not fast food, then I don't know what is.

SERVES 2 TO 4

2 squab

FOR THE MARINADE
2 garlic cloves, minced
2 tablespoons dried marjoram
1 tablespoon coriander seeds, toasted
   and ground (see Tip on page 15)
1 teaspoon chile flakes

1 teaspoon ground black pepper
3 tablespoons olive oil
juice of ½ lemon
sea salt flakes

TO SERVE
bread
arugula salad

Line a baking pan with nonstick parchment paper.

To spatchcock the squab, place each bird in turn breast-side down on a cutting board. Using a pair of poultry shears, cut down either side of the backbone and then remove the bone. Lay the bird breast-side up on the prepared baking pan and gently press down on each one with both hands until as flat as possible.

Mix all the marinade ingredients together in a small bowl or measuring cup, then pour it over the squab and rub in all over. Cover the pan with plastic wrap and place in the refrigerator to marinate for 1 hour, or overnight, if liked.

Preheat the oven to 425°F.

Roast the birds for about 30 minutes until cooked through and nicely browned with crispy skin (the juices should run clear when the thickest part of the meat is pierced with the tip of a sharp knife). Remove from the oven and let rest for 10 minutes before serving with bread and an arugula salad.

SIMPLY DELICIOUS WITH...

Mashed Cannellini Beans with Preserved Lemon & Tahini (see page 31) or Roasted Parsnips with Tahini Yogurt Sauce, Herb Oil & Pomegranate Seeds (see page 177).

Pomegranate molasses & honey-glazed meatballs

Essentially, these meatballs are a total spice-cupboard raid, but what really brings them to life and sets them apart from other recipes I've written is the finish of pomegranate molasses. It's an ingredient that works so well with red meat and game, as it cuts through any richness effortlessly and makes for such a wonderful and somewhat exotic flavor combination. I have always drizzled pomegranate molasses onto tomatoes, salads, kebabs, and grilled meats, so it was only a matter of time before I paired it with meatballs, too.

MAKES ABOUT 24 TO 28 MEATBALLS

1lb 2oz ground beef (20% fat)

1 onion, minced in a food processor and drained of any liquid, or very finely chopped

1 small pack (about 1oz) of flat leaf parsley, finely chopped

1 tablespoon garlic granules

1 teaspoon ground cumin

1 teaspoon ground coriander

1 teaspoon ground cinnamon

1 teaspoon sea salt flakes, crumbled

vegetable oil, for frying

FOR THE GLAZE

¼ cup pomegranate molasses

2 tablespoons liquid honey

Put all the main ingredients, except the vegetable oil, into a large mixing bowl and, using your hands, work them together really well, pummeling the meat mixture for several minutes into a smooth paste.

Line a plate with paper towels. Shape the mixture into 24 to 28 evenly-sized meatballs.

Heat a large skillet over medium-high heat. Once the skillet is hot, add a drizzle of vegetable oil and fry the meatballs in batches for 8 to 10 minutes until browned all over and cooked through. Remove from the pan with a slotted spoon and transfer to the lined plate to drain.

Wipe the pan with paper towels and return it to the stove over medium heat. Mix the pomegranate molasses and honey for the glaze together. Return the meatballs to the pan and add the glaze. Roll the meatballs in the glaze to coat. Cook until the glaze has reduced to a sticky coating. Serve immediately.

SIMPLY DELICIOUS WITH...

Tomato & Garlic Rice (see page 38) or Polow-e-Bademjan-o-Felfel (see page 125).

Pot-roasted brisket
with harissa & spices

One-pot cooking is a joy, and this little beauty never disappoints. From a cook's perspective, nothing could be easier than this recipe, and from the diner's perspective, it's ridiculously juicy, tender, and packs in plenty of flavor. Should you, for some unknown reason, have any left over, it makes a wonderful sandwich, meatpie filling, or a stew. Or, combine any leftovers with a can of coconut milk and serve over rice for the most rewarding bowl of comfort the next day.

SERVES 6 TO 8

3 cups cold water

2 heaped tablespoons rose harissa

1 teaspoon ground turmeric

1 teaspoon ground cumin

1 teaspoon ground cinnamon

1 teaspoon ground fenugreek

5½lb rolled beef brisket

sea salt flakes and freshly ground
   black pepper

Preheat the oven to 340°F.

Measure the cold water in a 1-quart measuring cup, add the harissa and ground spices along with a generous amount of salt and pepper, and stir until the ingredients are evenly combined.

Place the beef in an ovenproof casserole dish with a lid or a dutch oven and pour the spiced liquid over it. Cook, uncovered, for about 2 hours, basting regularly.

Cover the dish with the lid and cook for a further 2 hours, again basting the meat from time to time. Then remove the lid and cook the beef for a further 1 hour before serving.

SIMPLY DELICIOUS WITH...

Pomegranate Shallots (see page 27) and Spiced Turmeric Mashed Potatoes with Cilantro (see page 37).

TIP
This is fabulous with mashed root vegetables or shredded up and served with flatbread, yogurt, and a dash of pomegranate molasses, pomegranate seeds, and some fresh herbs, such as mint.

Smoky beef, potato & pea pan-fry
with eggs & yogurt

Every once in a while, laziness prevails and I want something that can be made and served in the skillet, and placed in the center of the table to be shared. I like to take the time to fry the potatoes properly, as they really are the star of the show.

SERVES 4

1¼lb potatoes, peeled and cut into ¾-inch cubes

vegetable oil, for frying

1 heaped teaspoon cumin seeds

1 onion, minced

1lb 2oz ground beef

1 teaspoon garlic granules

1 teaspoon smoked paprika

1 teaspoon ground turmeric

1 teaspoon sumac

2 handfuls of frozen peas

1 small pack (about 1oz) of flat leaf parsley, coarsely chopped

4 eggs

sea salt flakes and freshly ground black pepper

TO SERVE

Greek or plain yogurt

your favorite chile sauce (optional)

Rinse the potato cubes in cold water, drain well, and pat dry.

Line a plate with a double layer of paper towels. Heat a skillet over medium-high heat and pour in enough oil to coat the bottom of the skillet. Add the potatoes, spreading them out into a single layer, and fry for about 12 to 15 minutes until cooked through, turning the pieces over as they cook to ensure they all brown evenly and adding the cumin seeds once a couple of sides have browned. Remove with a slotted spoon and transfer to the lined plate to drain.

Add the onion to the skillet and fry for a few minutes until nicely browned, then add the ground beef and mix with the onion. Stir in the garlic granules, spices, and some salt and pepper and cook for a few minutes until the beef is cooked through. Add the frozen peas and cook, stirring, for a few minutes. Then stir through the parsley and the fried potatoes. Next, make 4 wells in the mixture and crack an egg into each. Cover the pan with a lid and cook for 5 to 7 minutes, or until the eggs are cooked to your liking. Season with black pepper, then serve straight from the skillet with Greek or plain yogurt and your favorite chile sauce, if liked.

Yogurt & spice roasted salmon

I love cooking salmon in the oven. It's lazy, quick, and works really well. You don't really need to add any oil, as salmon is naturally fatty and delicious. These little salmon bites are something I've made time and again over the years and the method of roasting them at a high temperature ensures you get a little charring on the outside yet perfectly cooked salmon on the inside. Leftovers also make a great addition to your lunchbox the next day.

SERVES 4

1lb 2oz skinless salmon fillet, cut into 1½-inch cubes

FOR THE MARINADE

¼ cup Greek yogurt

1 tablespoon garlic granules

1 heaped tablespoon rose harissa

1 teaspoon ground turmeric

1 teaspoon paprika

finely grated zest of 1 lime and a good squeeze of juice

1 teaspoon olive oil

generous amount of sea salt flakes and freshly ground black pepper

TO SERVE

tortilla wraps

sliced tomatoes

finely sliced onion

cilantro leaves

Greek yogurt

Preheat your oven to its highest setting. Line a baking pan with nonstick parchment paper.

Stir all the marinade ingredients to combine in a mixing bowl. Add the salmon cubes and turn them over in the marinade to coat.

Spread the salmon out on the prepared baking pan and roast for 10 minutes until cooked through. Remove from the oven and serve immediately with tortilla wraps, tomatoes, finely sliced onion, cilantro leaves, and Greek yogurt.

SIMPLY DELICIOUS WITH…

Maast-o-Esfenaj (see page 72) or Baked Sweet Potato Fries with Za'atar & Garlic (see page 34).

Sea bream
with spiced green olive & shallot butter

As a child, I wasn't always the biggest lover of fish. It might be a Persian thing, since fish doesn't tend to feature heavily in the traditional Persian diet, unless you live by the sea. This may explain why we can be tricky to please. These days I am crazy about fish of every description; the older I get, the more I enjoy it and tend to choose it when eating out. It is light, digestible, and an excellent carrier of flavor, so long as you don't overpower a delicate variety. Sea bream is one that can handle a little flavor bomb, and this simple but effective spiced butter is just that—an explosion of flavor that just works incredibly well with the fish.

SERVES 2 TO 4

¼ cup olive oil

4 skin-on sea bream fillets, about
  3½oz each

3½ tablespoons butter

16 green olives, pitted and
  finely chopped

1 small shallot, minced

1 heaped teaspoon sumac

1 heaped teaspoon pul biber
  chile flakes

sea salt flakes and freshly ground
  black pepper

Heat a skillet over medium-high heat. Once hot, drizzle in 1 tablespoon of the olive oil, add 2 sea bream fillets, skin-side down, and fry for 2 to 3 minutes until the skin crisps up, then carefully turn them over and cook for a further minute. Remove from the skillet and keep warm under foil. Repeat with the remaining sea bream fillets.

Wipe the skillet with paper towels and place on very low heat. Add the remaining 2 tablespoons of olive oil and then the butter. Once melted, add the olives and shallot. Stir for 1 to 2 minutes to heat through gently. Season generously with salt and pepper, then add the sumac and the pul biber and stir well. Pour the spiced butter evenly over the fish and serve immediately.

SIMPLY DELICIOUS WITH...

Mashed Cannellini Beans with Preserved Lemon & Tahini (see page 31) and Charred Zucchini with Lemon, Oregano & Pul Biber (see page 28).

Beet & feta lattice

It's no secret that I always keep vacuum-packed cooked beets and feta cheese in my refrigerator at all times. They have saved me from going hungry on many occasions and are actually rather wonderful when paired together, especially in salads. But sometimes, and especially in winter, you want something warm and comforting, so you might say this recipe is inevitable when you also find yourself with a spare package of puff pastry. That perfect balance of a sweet, salty, and creamy filling encased in flaky pastry is comfort food personified. Hot or cold, side dish or main, it's a winner.

SERVES 4 TO 6

14oz vacuum-packed cooked beets in natural juice (or peeled, cooked, whole fresh beets)

1 heaped teaspoon dried wild oregano

1 teaspoon chile flakes

10½oz vegetarian feta cheese

1 x 11oz ready-rolled all-butter puff pastry sheet

beaten egg, to glaze

freshly ground black pepper

Preheat the oven to 400°F. Line a baking pan with nonstick parchment paper.

For the filling, coarsely grate the beets. Place in a sieve and squeeze out as much of the juice as you can without crushing the beets. Tip into a mixing bowl with the oregano, chile flakes, and a generous amount of pepper, then loosely crumble in the feta and give everything a good mix.

Cut the pastry sheet lengthwise in half into 2 long rectangles, one for bottom of the lattice and one for the top. Lay the pastry bottom on the prepared baking pan and spoon the filling down its length, then use your hands to neatly pack and compress the filling into a sausage shape, leaving a ½-inch border of clear pastry.

Make a series of small diagonal cuts in 3 evenly spaced rows running down the other piece of pastry (or cut an alternative pattern of your choosing), leaving a 1¼-inch border of uncut pastry. Place this piece of pastry over the filling, carefully stretching it out to cover everything. Then tuck the edges underneath the pastry on the bottom to neaten and hide the seam. Press the edges down firmly, then brush beaten egg over all the exposed pastry. Bake for 25 to 30 minutes, or until the pastry is deep golden brown. Remove from the oven, cut into slices, and serve immediately, or serve cold.

SIMPLY DELICIOUS WITH...

Pear, Chickpea & Green Leaf Salad with Maple Harissa Dressing (see page 172).

Roasted nectarines
with labneh, herbs & honey

Is this a salad? Is it a dessert? The truth is, I just don't know. One thing I do know for sure is that it's absolutely delicious. It's a dish that people circle around apprehensively not knowing how to tackle it, but once they do, it's gone pretty quickly. Fruity, savory, crunchy, spicy, and sweet, it's the kind of combination that simply cannot fail to please.

SERVES 4 TO 6

4 large ripe nectarines, halved
  and stoned

olive oil, for drizzling

1lb 2oz labneh, or 2 cups Greek
  yogurt strained in a cheesecloth
  bag overnight (see page 11)

generous handful of toasted flaked
  almonds

1 heaped teaspoon dried wild oregano

1 heaped teaspoon pul biber chile flakes

2 tablespoons liquid honey

handful of mint leaves, stacked, rolled up
  together, and finely sliced widthwise
  into thin ribbons

sea salt flakes and freshly ground
  black pepper

Preheat the oven to 425°F. Line a large baking pan with nonstick parchment paper.

Place the nectarine halves cut-side up on the prepared pan, then drizzle each with a little olive oil and season generously with pepper. Bake for 25 to 30 minutes until the edges of the fruit are brown and the flesh is cooked through and tender. Remove from the oven and let cool.

Select a large serving plate and spread the labneh or strained Greek yogurt all over the surface. Arrange the roasted nectarines on top. Drizzle with a little olive oil, season with a little salt, and sprinkle with the toasted flaked almonds, followed by the oregano and pul biber. Drizzle with the honey and, finally, scatter with the mint ribbons. Take to the table to serve.

SIMPLY DELICIOUS WITH...

Lamb & Mint Kofte (see page 78) or Spiced Belgian Endive & Roasted Bell Pepper Salad with Oranges & Anchovies (see page 180).

Traditions
with a twist

Maast-o-esfenaj
spinach & yogurt with walnuts

This is a much-loved staple of Persian cuisine. Traditionally, we don't add garlic or sumac, and walnuts may be used to garnish the top, but I like to add them to the dish for texture. This is the one dish that always surprises my students at my Persian cookery class. Yogurt is always thought of as a dip in the West. Persians treat it as a main event but also as a condiment that goes with or over everything. It is even enjoyed on its own.

SERVES 6 TO 8

9oz spinach leaves

2 cups thick Greek yogurt

1 large garlic clove, minced

2 generous handfuls of walnut
halves, coarsely chopped

2 teaspoons sumac, plus extra to garnish

olive oil, for drizzling

sea salt flakes and freshly ground
black pepper

flatbread, to serve

Bring a saucepan of water to a boil, add the spinach, and let simmer for 2 to 3 minutes until wilted. Then drain and plunge into a bowl of iced water to stop it from cooking further. Once cooled, drain well and finely chop.

Put the spinach into a mixing bowl with the yogurt, garlic, walnuts (reserving some for garnish), sumac, a little drizzle of olive oil, and a generous amount of salt and pepper. Mix together well.

Spread the mixture out on a flat plate, then drizzle with olive oil and sprinkle with extra sumac and the reserved walnuts before serving.

SIMPLY DELICIOUS WITH...
Yogurt & Spice Roasted Salmon (see page 62) or Tepsi Kebap (see page 84).

Butternut borani

Very few Persian meals are enjoyed without yogurt in some shape or form, and the most popular dishes are yogurt with cucumber, spinach, or Persian wild garlic (which is different from the leafy wild garlic or ramsons found in British woodlands). A student once came to my cookery class and told me that the region where her family are from use squash to make a yogurt dish, so I had to try it for myself. It is insanely delicious and always the first item to be finished whenever I serve it. People are often so surprised it's made from butternut squash.

SERVES 4 TO 6

2¾lb butternut squash

olive oil, for drizzling

2 garlic cloves, minced

1¼ cups Greek yogurt

½ small pack (about ½oz) of dill weed, very finely chopped

1 teaspoon pul biber chile flakes

handful of walnut pieces

sea salt flakes and freshly ground black pepper

flatbread, to serve

Preheat the oven to 425°F. Line a baking pan with nonstick parchment paper.

Leaving the skin on, cut the butternut squash in half lengthwise and, using a spoon, scoop out the seeds and discard. Place the squash halves cut-side up on the prepared baking pan and rub the exposed flesh with a little drizzle of olive oil. Roast for about 45 to 50 minutes, then insert a knife into the thickest part of the flesh to check if it's soft and cooked through. If or when the squash is cooked, remove from the oven and set aside until cool enough to handle.

Using a spoon, scoop all the squash flesh out of the skins into a mixing bowl, then mash as best as you can. Add the garlic, a drizzle of olive oil, and a generous amount of salt and pepper, followed by the yogurt, and give everything a good stir. Check and adjust the seasoning, then transfer the borani to a plate. Spread it right to the edges and smooth it over with the back of the spoon. Drizzle with olive oil and scatter with the pul biber, dill weed, and, finally, the walnuts before serving with flatbread.

SIMPLY DELICIOUS WITH...
Harissa Chicken Noodle Lettuce Cups (see page 115) or Sticky Harissa, Sesame & Pistachio Chicken (see page 147).

Green hummus

This is a very different hummus flavorwise from the traditional variety. I really love the vibrant color but the punchy combination of herbs also gives it a unique taste that pairs really well with crudités, lettuce leaves, and pitta bread. It's also perfect as a filling for sandwiches and wraps alike. Mostly, though, I like to dip raw carrots into it, as their sweetness works really well with it. But then again, for a girl like me, hummus can always be eaten on its own by the heaped spoonful.

SERVES 6 TO 8

2 x 14oz cans chickpeas, drained and ¾ of the brine of 1 can reserved

juice of ½ lemon, or more to taste

2 garlic cloves, peeled

1 small pack (about 1oz) of flat leaf parsley

1 small pack (about 1oz) of fresh cilantro

½ small pack (about ½oz) of tarragon, leaves picked

2 tablespoons tahini

generous amount of sea salt flakes and freshly ground black pepper

pitta bread, to serve

TO GARNISH

1 teaspoon nigella seeds

olive oil

Put all the main ingredients into a blender (if using a food processor, you will need to mince the garlic and coarsely chop the herbs first) and blitz until smooth.

Check and adjust the seasoning, adding more lemon juice to taste. Serve garnished with the nigella seeds and a drizzle of olive oil.

SIMPLY DELICIOUS WITH...

Fragrant Fish Cakes with Preserved Lemon Mayonnaise (see page 152) or Crispy Shrimp with Mango & Tomato Dip (see page 164).

Lamb & mint kofte

These simple yet delicious little kofte are based on something I tasted in a restaurant in Antakya (the ancient Roman city of Antioch in southern Turkey). The recipe calls for dried mint, which is a wonderfully versatile ingredient in cooking. These kofte really are pleasingly straightforward and I've made them many times since coming back from that trip.

MAKES ABOUT 20

1lb 2oz ground lamb
1 onion, minced in a food processor
    and drained of any liquid, or very
    finely chopped
2 tablespoons dried mint
2 eggs
vegetable oil, for frying
generous amount of sea salt flakes
    and freshly ground black pepper

TO SERVE
Greek or plain yogurt
chopped fresh mint leaves

Put all the main ingredients, except the vegetable oil, into a large mixing bowl and, using your hands, work them together really well, pummeling the meat mixture for several minutes into a smooth, even paste.

Take golf-ball-sized amounts of the mixture and shape into round patties, about 20 in total.

Heat a large skillet over medium-high heat. Once hot, drizzle in a little vegetable oil and cook the patties in batches for 3 to 4 minutes on each side until browned on both sides and cooked through. Thread each patty onto a little wooden skewer and serve with a bowl of Greek or plain yogurt scattered with some chopped fresh mint for dipping.

SIMPLY DELICIOUS WITH...
Flame-roasted Bell Pepper, Pistachio & Dill Weed Yogurt (see page 42) or Maast-o-Esfenaj (see page 72).

TIP
Keep the first batch of patties warm covered in foil while you cook the second batch, then reheat them in the pan if necessary.

Ultimate falafels

These falafel are less traditional and more Sabrina style, packed with herbs and bolstered with extra flavor. But the result is every bit as satisfying.

MAKES 20 TO 25

1¼ cups dried chickpeas

1 cup flat leaf parsley,
    coarsely chopped

1¼ cups fresh cilantro,
    coarsely chopped

1 large carrot, scrubbed and grated

2 large garlic cloves, minced

4 fat scallions, very thinly sliced

1 onion, minced

2 tablespoons all-purpose flour

1 teaspoon baking powder

1 tablespoon ground coriander

1 teaspoon ground turmeric

vegetable oil, for deep-frying

sea salt flakes and freshly ground
    black pepper

TO SERVE

pitta bread, sliced gherkins, sliced
    tomatoes, sliced red cabbage,
    Greek or plain yogurt (or vegan
    alternative), chile sauce

Soak the chickpeas in cold water overnight, or for 8 to 10 hours, then drain.

Put the chickpeas along with all the remaining main ingredients, except the vegetable oil, into a food processor and season generously with salt and pepper. Blitz until evenly combined but still slightly coarse in texture (don't worry too much about the consistency).

Pour enough oil into a deep skillet or saucepan to fill to a depth of about 1½ inches. Place over medium heat and bring to frying temperature. When it is hot but not smoking add a pinch of mixture. If it sizzles immediately, the oil is hot enough. Line a plate with paper towels.

Roll scoops of the mixture into smooth balls about 1½ inches in diameter. Fry the falafels in batches, a few at a time without overcrowding the pan, for 2 to 3 minutes, or until just starting to brown all over. Remove with a slotted spoon and transfer to the lined plate to drain. Serve hot in pitta bread with pickled cucumbers, tomatoes, Greek or plain yogurt, and chile sauce.

SIMPLY DELICIOUS WITH...
Thyme & Za'atar Roasted Tomatoes with Strained Yogurt Balls (see page 11).

TIP
You really need dried chickpeas for this recipe. Don't be tempted to substitute the canned variety as they will result in mushy falafels.

Kabab koobideh

For Persians, this dish is an institution. The word "kebab" (or *kabab*, as Persians call it) means "to grill," usually over fire. The first kebabs were made by Persian soldiers who would grill meats on their swords, hence the traditional flat, sword-like skewers Persians use today. You can buy them online if you want to serve them this way yourself. Although we only have a few different varieties of kebab, for me, this is simplest yet most delicious.

MAKES 5 TO 6 LARGE KEBABS OR 10 TO 12 SMALL PATTIES

2¼lb minced lamb (30% fat is essential)

2 large onions, minced in a food processor and drained of any liquid, or very finely chopped

2 level tablespoons ground turmeric

2 teaspoons baking soda

sea salt flakes and freshly ground black pepper

6 tomatoes

flatbread, to serve

Put all the main ingredients into a large mixing bowl and, using your hands, work them together really well, pummeling the meat mixture for several minutes into a smooth paste.

To make large kebabs, divide the mixture into 5 to 6 portions and form each portion around a flat sword skewer about 10 inches long. Using your thumb and forefinger, pinch the meat widthwise from one end of the kebab to the other to create the classic ridges. Cook them along with the whole tomatoes on a charcoal barbecue that has been burning for about 30 minutes. The trick is to cook them for about 10 to 15 minutes in total until the meat is browned and cooked through, while turning them every 2 minutes to help the fat render and to stop them from burning. Note that if they do start to burn, your barbecue is too hot.

To make small kebabs, preheat your oven to its highest setting. Line a large baking pan with nonstick parchment paper. Divide the mixture into 10 to 12 portions, form into sausages, then flatten and pinch as above to create ridges. Place on the prepared baking pan with the tomatoes and bake for 10 to 12 minutes.

Serve the kebabs and tomatoes immediately on flatbreads so the bread absorbs the lovely juices.

SIMPLY DELICIOUS WITH...
Naan-o-Paneer-o-Sabzi (see page 108).

TIP
This recipe only works if you use ground meat containing 30 percent fat or more—it plays a vital part in keeping the kebab juicy and bursting with flavor.

Tepsi kebap

What the Turks don't know about making kebabs just isn't worth knowing. *Tepsi* is the Turkish word for "tray," which is what this recipe is traditionally cooked in, and *kebap* is the Turkish word for "kebab." I visited a butcher's shop attached to a restaurant in Antakya in Turkey and was roped into hand-mincing the ingredients for this recipe using a giant machete-like knife. The mixture was then pressed into a baking pan and baked in a wood-fired oven. The results were spectacular, and the flavor so memorable I came back home and created a version in a shallow casserole dish. If any one recipe changes the way you cook, this may just be it. The meat is juicy, tender, and charred on top, and the ease of pressing the meat into the dish makes this a super-simple way to cook a kebab.

SERVES 4 TO 6

1lb 2oz ground lamb (20% fat)

1 onion, minced in a food processor and drained of any liquid, or very finely chopped

2 large garlic cloves, minced

½ red bell pepper, cored, seeded, and very finely chopped

1 cup flat leaf parsley, leaves and stalks finely chopped, plus extra leaves to serve

2 tablespoons tomato paste

1 tablespoon pul biber chile flakes

½ teaspoon baking soda

generous amount of sea salt flakes and freshly ground black pepper

TO SERVE

tortilla wraps or bread

sliced red onion

Greek yogurt, optional

Preheat your oven to its highest setting. Select an ovenproof dish or baking pan (I use a shallow cast-iron casserole dish about 8½ inches in diameter).

Put all the main ingredients into a large mixing bowl and, using your hands, work them together well, pummeling the meat mixture for several minutes into a smooth, even paste.

Press the meat mixture into the ovenproof dish or baking pan to cover the bottom. Bake for 18 minutes, or until golden on top. Serve immediately with tortilla wraps or bread, some sliced red onion, parsley leaves, and Greek yogurt, if liked.

SIMPLY DELICIOUS WITH...
Tomato & Garlic Rice (see page 38) or Maast-o-Esfenaj (see page 72).

Tahchin

Forced by my mother to learn and perfect *tahchin*, I finally achieved a version that I think retains the authentic qualities of this classic baked rice cake while paring it down to make it achievable for anyone who wants to give it a try. Barberries are key to this recipe. Persians love frying these sour little berries in butter and sugar to create a layer in the center and sometimes garnish the top with a generous quantity, too. I've kept this recipe simple by sticking to the middle layer only, which gives the most wonderfully sharp yet sweet and fruity tang sandwiched between two layers of saffron-scented rice. In essence, this dish is truly spectacular and a comforting family favorite of mine.

SERVES 6 TO 8

2 ¼ cups basmati rice

olive oil, for frying

1 large onion, halved and thinly sliced
    into half moons

1lb 2oz boneless, skinless chicken
    thighs, cut into ½-inch cubes

1 stick of butter

1 ¼ cups Greek yogurt

a small pinch of saffron threads, ground
    to a powder using a mortar and
    pestle, then steeped in ⅓ cup boiling
    water until cool

3 eggs

5 ½oz dried barberries

¼ cup superfine sugar

melted ghee or vegetable oil,
    for oiling

sea salt flakes and freshly ground
    black pepper

Bring a large saucepan of water to a boil. Add the rice and stir to stop the grains from sticking together. Parboil for about 6 to 7 minutes until the grains turn from a dullish off-white color to a more opaque, brilliant white and have slightly elongated but are still firm to the bite. Drain and immediately rinse thoroughly under cold running water, running your fingers through the rice, until all the grains are well rinsed of starch and completely cooled. Drain the rice thoroughly by shaking the sieve well, then let stand over the sink to allow any remaining water to drain away. Shake off any excess water before use.

CONTINUED OVERLEAF

Place a small saucepan over medium heat, drizzle in a little olive oil, and add the onion. Cook for a few minutes until softened and translucent. Add the chicken and mix into the onion, then cook over very low heat for 30 minutes until cooked through and tender.

Preheat the oven to 400°F.

Once the chicken is done, add half the butter, and as soon as it melts, remove the pan from the heat and mix through. Transfer the contents of the pan to a large mixing bowl. Add the parboiled rice, yogurt, saffron solution, and eggs. Mix thoroughly until evenly combined. Season generously with salt and pepper and mix again.

Place a skillet over medium heat and add the remaining butter. Once it has melted, add the barberries and then the sugar. Stir to coat the barberries in the sugar and butter mixture. As soon as the sugar dissolves, immediately remove the pan from the heat, otherwise the sugar will crystallize.

Line a 13 x 8-inch ovenproof dish with nonstick parchment paper and brush with melted ghee or vegetable oil (if using a nonstick dish, just brush with melted ghee or oil). Pour half the rice mixture into the dish and shake it to compress the rice and ensure it is in an even layer. Scatter the barberries on top to cover the surface and pour the remaining rice mixture over them. Smooth the top and bake on the lowest rack of the oven for 1 hour and 20 to 30 minutes.

Once cooked, place a tray or platter over the dish and carefully invert the tahchin onto it, then serve immediately.

SIMPLY DELICIOUS WITH...
Green-yogurt-dressed Baby Romaine Lettuce with Burnt Hazelnuts (see page 44) or Maast-o-Esfenaj (see page 72).

Albaloo polow

This classic Persian rice dish of lamb and sour cherry meatballs best showcases our long-standing historic culinary tradition of combining meat with fruits. You could try it with ground beef instead of ground lamb, and substitute sweetened cranberries if you can't find sour cherries. You can also omit the meatballs and serve the polow with a roast chicken or just on its own, but the meatballs were my favorite bit as a child.

SERVES 6 TO 8

1lb 2oz ground lamb (20% fat)

1 onion, minced in a food processor and drained of any liquid, or very finely chopped

1 tablespoon garlic granules

vegetable oil, for frying

2¼ cups basmati rice

1¾ cups boiling water

14oz sweetened dried Morello or sour cherries (or use sweetened dried cranberries)

2 tablespoons ghee

sea salt flakes and freshly ground black pepper

Put the ground lamb, onion, garlic granules, and a generous amount of salt and pepper into a mixing bowl and, using your hands, work the ingredients together really well, pummeling the meat mixture for several minutes into a smooth, even paste. Roll the mixture into balls ¾ inch in diameter to make about 40 in total.

Heat a large skillet over high heat. Line a plate with a double layer of paper towels. Once the pan is hot, drizzle in a little vegetable oil and fry the meatballs in 2 batches until browned all over. Remove from the pan with a slotted spoon and transfer to the lined plate to drain.

Bring a large, ideally nonstick, saucepan of salted water to a boil. Add the rice and stir to stop the grains from sticking together. Parboil for about 6 to 7 minutes until the grains turn from a dullish off-white color to a more opaque, brilliant white and have slightly elongated. Drain and immediately rinse thoroughly under cold running water, running your fingers through the rice, until all the grains are well rinsed of starch and completely cool. Drain the rice thoroughly by giving the sieve a good shake and then standing it over the sink to allow any remaining water to drain away. Shake off any excess water before use.

CONTINUED OVERLEAF

Meanwhile, pour the boiling water into a small saucepan and place over medium heat. Add the sour cherries and boil for several minutes, stirring frequently, until the liquid turns syrupy enough to coat the back of a spoon (see Tip).

Rinse the rice saucepan and place over very low heat. If the pan isn't nonstick, first line the bottom with a large square of nonstick parchment paper (see Tip on page 102). Add the ghee and, once melted, pour in enough cold water to come ½ inch up the inside of the pan. Swirl the pan around to mix the ghee and water together, then add a generous amount of crushed salt flakes. Loosely scatter just enough rice into the pan to cover the bottom in an even layer (don't pack the mixture into the pan), then mix the rest of the rice with the cherries and meatballs to combine. Scatter (do not press) the rice mixture into the pan, allowing for natural air pockets, then smooth it out to the sides. Using the handle of a wooden spoon, poke a series of holes into the rice, piercing all the way to the bottom of the pan (this allows the steam to circulate). Wrap the pan lid in a clean dish cloth so that it fits tightly onto the pan. If using a gas stove, cook over the lowest flame for 1 hour. If using an electric/induction stove, cook over medium heat for 20 minutes, then reduce the heat to medium-low and cook for a further 1½ to 2 hours.

Once cooked, remove the lid and smooth the rice over the edges to level it off. Place a large platter over the pan and carefully flip the polow onto it to reveal the crispy *tahdig* crust. Don't be disheartened if it is dark. This is caused by the dark cherry juice which, being sweet, has a tendency to caramelize. It can appear blackened even though it has not actually burnt.

SIMPLY DELICIOUS WITH...
Maast-o-Esfenaj (see page 72) or Cucumber, Green Apple & Nigella Salad with Feta & Dill Weed (see page 48).

TIP
If your cherries have too much liquid around them, boil until reduced, otherwise they will make the rice too wet and juice will seep to the bottom and burn the crust.

Tahdig e Makaroni

This dish is an absolute Persian classic. The pasta is given the same *tahdig* (crispy crust) treatment as our rice dishes, making it chewy, crunchy, and out of this world. Not remotely Italian, but a much-loved Persian staple that you need to try at least once.

SERVES 6

1lb 2oz spaghetti

olive oil , for frying

1 large onion, very finely chopped

1lb 2oz ground beef

1 heaped teaspoon ground turmeric

1 heaped teaspoon garlic granules

¾ cup tomato paste

1 cup cold water

1 heaping teaspoon sugar

2 tablespoons butter

2 tablespoons ghee or vegetable oil

sea salt flakes and black pepper

Cook the spaghetti in a large saucepan of salted boiling water following the package directions. Drain and rinse under cold running water, then drain again and set aside.

Place a large skillet over medium heat and pour in enough olive oil to coat the bottom of the pan. Add the onion and cook for a few minutes until beginning to brown, then add the ground beef and mix it with the onion. Stir in the turmeric, garlic granules, tomato paste, and a generous amount of salt and pepper (the mixture will need overseasoning at this stage).

Increase the heat and cook until the meat browns, then add the cold water and sugar and mix well. Cook until most of the water has evaporated, stirring occasionally to stop it from sticking to the pan, then remove from the heat. Stir in the butter to create a glossy sauce, then set aside.

Place a nonstick saucepan over very low heat. If your pan isn't nonstick, first line the bottom with a square of nonstick parchment paper (see Tip on page 102). Add the ghee and season with salt. Once the ghee has melted, pour in enough cold water to come ½ inch up the inside of the pan. Swirl the pan around to mix the ghee and water together. Add 2 handfuls of the cooked spaghetti to the pan to cover the bottom generously. Mix the remaining spaghetti with the meat sauce, then pour it all into the pan and cover with a lid. If using a gas stove, cook over the lowest flame for 1 hour. If using an electric/induction stove, cook over medium heat for 20 minutes, then reduce the heat to medium-low and cook for a further 1½ hours.

Once cooked, remove the lid, place a large platter over the pan, and carefully invert the makaroni onto it to serve. No accompaniment needed.

Maman Malek's Borscht

You may be surprised to hear that this is my grandmother's recipe, especially since she spent so little time cooking when I was a child. She absolutely hated being in the kitchen, but once in a blue moon she would prepare a meal and borscht was one among her limited repertoire. Iran and Russia often enjoyed friendly relations through history, so we do have some Russian-influenced dishes in our cuisine. Of course, our versions may be wildly different from the originals, but they have cemented my love for all kinds of Russian dishes today.

SERVES 4 TO 6

3 tablespoons vegetable oil

2 small onions, halved and sliced into thin half moons

1lb 5oz bone-in beef foreshank (about 2 steaks)

3 to 4 small oxtail pieces (about 9oz total weight)

1 heaped teaspoon coriander seeds

1lb 2oz red beets, scrubbed and grated

¾lb red cabbage, finely shredded

sea salt flakes and freshly ground black pepper

TO SERVE

½ cup Greek or plain yogurt

½ small pack (about ½ oz) of dill weed, chopped, optional

Place a large saucepan over medium heat and pour in the vegetable oil. Add the onions and cook for a few minutes until softened and translucent, then add the beef foreshank, the oxtail, a very generous amount of pepper (about 1 tablespoon), and the coriander seeds. Stir until the meat is well coated in the onions and spices. Seal the meat on both sides but without letting it brown.

Add the beets and cabbage, pour over enough cold water to cover all the ingredients, and season generously with salt. Stir well, then reduce the heat to medium-low and gently simmer for 30 minutes.

Skim the scum from the surface of the borscht and continue to cook uncovered for another 30 minutes. Then cover with a lid and simmer for a further 3½ to 4½ hours until the meat is tender and falls apart (remove the lid for the final 30 minutes of cooking time). Serve with the Greek or plain yogurt and dill weed.

Turmeric & black pepper braised lamb neck

Persians traditionally make this recipe as an accompaniment to a fava bean and dill weed rice dish, but they usually use lamb shanks. I do love lamb shanks but they can be quite expensive and aren't always easy to find. I taught this version of a classic recipe at my cookery classes and was surprised by how much people loved it and they way they treated it more like a stew. So, I decided it was high time I shared it with you.

SERVES 6

vegetable oil, for frying

2 large onions, halved and thinly sliced into half moons

4 fat garlic cloves, bashed and thinly sliced

1¾lb lamb neck fillets, cut into 1-inch chunks

2 heaped teaspoons ground turmeric

1 heaped teaspoon coarsely ground black pepper

2 heaped teaspoons sea salt flakes, crushed

rice, to serve

Place a large saucepan over medium-high heat and pour in enough vegetable oil to coat the bottom of the pan. Add the onions and cook for a few minutes until softened and translucent, without coloring, then stir in the garlic and cook for a few minutes.

Add the lamb, turmeric, and pepper and stir until the chunks of meat are well coated in the onion mixture. Seal the meat on all sides but without browning.

Add the salt, then pour in enough boiling water to just about cover the contents of the pan. Cover the pan with a lid, reduce the heat to low, and let simmer gently for 2½ hours. Check the pan every so often, giving the contents a stir and checking on the liquid level to ensure there is always just enough to barely cover the meat but also to allow the sauce to thicken a little and eventually reduce. About 30 minutes before the end of the cooking time, taste the sauce and season with more salt if necessary. Serve with rice.

SIMPLY DELICIOUS WITH...
Adas Polow (see page 101) or Polow-e Bademjan-o-Felfel (see page 125).

Koofteh berenji

I'm told this dish of lamb, rice, and yellow split-pea meatballs was my Grandpa Baba Ghayour's favorite thing to eat. He passed away when I was two, so this is one of my ways to remember him and keep his memory alive. My grandmother, who absolutely hated cooking, learned to make these knowing how much he loved them. If that's not love, then I don't know what is. This is the dish you want to come home to on a cold night—it is so comforting and delicoius—and is also perfect for batch freezing once cooked. You can also make them whatever size you fancy, big or small.

SERVES 6

¾ cup yellow split peas

¾ basmati rice

1lb 2oz ground lamb (20% fat)

1 small pack (about 1oz) of flat leaf parsley, finely chopped

1 small pack (about 1oz) of dill weed, finely chopped

1 small pack (about 1oz) of chives, finely snipped

1 small pack (about 1oz) of fresh cilantro, finely chopped

2 tablespoons all-purpose flour

3 teaspoons ground turmeric

generous pinch of saffron threads, ground to a powder using a mortar and pestle, then steeped in 3 tablespoons boiling water until cool

4 garlic cloves, minced

2 large onions, 1 minced in a food processor and drained of any liquid, or very finely chopped, and 1 halved and thinly sliced into half moons

2 handfuls of dried barberries

3 eggs

vegetable oil, for frying

1 heaping tablespoon tomato paste

14oz can chopped tomatoes

1 quart boiling water

sea salt flakes and freshly ground black pepper

TO SERVE
Greek or plain yogurt

flatbread

Bring a small saucepan of water to a boil and stir in a generous amount of crumbled salt flakes. Add the yellow split peas and stir, then reduce the heat to medium and let simmer for 25 minutes until the split peas are cooked. Drain and set aside to cool.

CONTINUED OVERLEAF

Refill the pan with water, bring to a boil, and stir in salt as before. Add the rice and stir to stop the grains from sticking together. Parboil for 7 minutes until the grains turn from a dullish off-white color to a more opaque, brilliant white and have slightly elongated. Drain and set aside to cool.

Put the cooled rice and split peas into a large mixing bowl with the lamb, herbs, flour, 2 teaspoons of the turmeric, the saffron solution, half the garlic, the minced or very finely chopped onion, the barberries, eggs, and a generous amount of salt and pepper. Mix together until evenly combined. Divide the mixture into 12 portions and then roll and compress each portion into a smooth ball.

Place a large saucepan over medium heat and pour in enough vegetable oil to coat the bottom of the pan. Add the sliced onion and fry gently for a few minutes until it begins to color slightly. Add the remaining garlic and gently fry for 2 to 3 minutes, then stir in the tomato paste and the remaining teaspoon of turmeric. Tip in the canned tomatoes, stir until evenly distributed and season with a generous amount of salt and pepper. Then pour in the measured boiling water and stir to mix.

Bring the sauce to a gentle boil and then add each koofteh (meatball) one at a time to the sauce. Partially cover the pan with a lid and let simmer for 20 minutes. Using 2 teaspoons, gently turn the meatballs over, then replace the pan lid as before and continue cooking for a further 30 to 45 minutes. Serve with yogurt and flatbread.

SIMPLY DELICIOUS WITH...
Maast-o-Esfenaj (see page 72) or Naan-o-Paneer-o-Sabzi (see page 108).

TIP
You can keep the meatballs cooking in the sauce over low heat for up to 1 hour, but just ensure the sauce doesn't reduce too much. It should be like soup in consistency, rather than a thick sauce.

Adas polow

This is one of the rice dishes that I loved as a child. My mother was never a big fan, but my grandmother absolutely adored it (though she rarely made it herself). Her love for it was infectious and so, in later life, I taught myself how to make it and began teaching it at my cookery classes with great success. Some people like to add chopped dates, but I find the combination of raisins, lentils, and saffron create the perfect balance.

SERVES 6 TO 8

1 cup uncooked green lentils

2½ cups basmati rice

2 tablespoons ghee

2 to 3 generous handfuls of raisins,
   to taste

2 pinches of saffron threads,
   finely crumbled

¾ stick butter, cut into small cubes

sea salt flakes

Parboil the lentils in a saucepan of salted boiling water for 15 minutes. Drain and rinse thoroughly under cold running water until cold, then drain again and set aside.

Bring a large, ideally nonstick, saucepan of salted water to a boil and stir in a generous handful of crumbled salt flakes. Add the rice and stir to stop the grains from sticking together. Parboil for about 6 to 7 minutes until the grains turn from a dullish off-white color to a more opaque, brilliant white, and have slightly elongated. Drain and immediately rinse thoroughly under cold running water, running your fingers through the rice, until all the grains are well rinsed of starch and completely cool. Drain the rice thoroughly by giving the sieve a good shake and standing it over the sink for 5 to 10 minutes so any remaining water can drain. Shake off any excess water before use, then tip into a large mixing bowl.

Rinse the saucepan and place over very low heat. If the pan isn't nonstick, line the bottom with a large square of nonstick parchment pape (see Tip overleaf). Add the ghee and, once melted, pour in enough cold water to come ½ inch up the inside of the pan. Swirl the pan around to mix the ghee and water together, then add a generous amount of crushed salt flakes.

CONTINUED OVERLEAF

Loosely scatter just enough rice into the pan to coat the bottom in an even layer (don't pack the mixture into the pan). Mix the raisins, lentils, and crumbled saffron into the remaining rice until evenly combined. Scatter (do not press) the rice mixture into the pan, allowing for natural air pockets, and smooth it out to the sides. Using the handle of a wooden spoon, poke a series of holes into the rice, piercing all the way to the bottom of the pan (this allows the steam to circulate), then dot the cubes of butter over the surface. Wrap the pan lid in a clean dish cloth so that it fits tightly on the pan. If using a gas stove, cook over the lowest flame for 1 hour. If using an electric/induction stove, cook over medium heat for 20 minutes, then reduce the heat to medium-low and cook for a further 1½ to 2 hours.

Once cooked, remove the lid and smooth the rice over to the edges to level it off. Place a large serving dish over the pan and carefully invert the polow onto it to reveal the crunchy *tahdig* crust. Alternatively, spoon out the rice, then scrape out the *tahdig* crust, and serve it on top of the rice. Just remember that the raisins contain sugar, so any that caught on the bottom of the pan may appear blackened, which is absolutely fine.

SIMPLY DELICIOUS WITH...
Spice-rubbed Spatchcocked Squab (see page 55).

TIP
If you crumple up the square of nonstick parchment paper and then smooth it out, this makes it more flexible and therefore easier to line the pan with.

Khoresh-e-karafs

This lamb, celery, and herb stew is one of my absolute favorite Persian *khoresh* (stew) recipes, and one I teach regularly at my Persian cookery classes. In this, the celery is tender, almost soft, and the stew is packed full of the fragrant dried mint and parsley, all immersed in a citrus-spiked meat broth. It freezes beautifully, so make things easy, double the batch, and freeze the rest for a rainy day. You won't regret it.

SERVES 6 TO 8

vegetable oil, for frying

1 bunch of celery, stalks separated and
    cut into 1¼-inch pieces

2 white onions, diced

1¾lb lamb neck fillet, cut widthwise
    into ¾-inch thick pieces

2 teaspoons ground turmeric

3 heaped tablespoons dried mint

7oz flat leaf parsley, coarsely chopped

juice of ½ lemon, or more to taste

sea salt flakes and freshly ground
    black pepper

basmati rice, to serve

Heat your largest saucepan over medium heat. Pour in enough vegetable oil to generously coat the bottom of the pan. Add the celery and cook for 20 to 30 minutes, stirring occasionally, until completely soft, without browning. The celery should lose its color and turn gray when cooked. Remove the celery with a slotted spoon and set aside. Return the pan to the heat, add the onions, and let them sweat in the leftover oil for a few minutes until softened and translucent, without browning. It's important not to brown the vegetables (or the meat, for that matter) as we don't want any brown coloring in this dish.

Add the lamb pieces and stir to coat them in the onion mixture, then add the turmeric and dried mint. Stir well until the meat is evenly coated. Next, add the parsley, and this is where you need to pay special attention. Cook for 20 to 30 minutes, stirring regularly and without browning the parsley, until it has completely wilted, reduced in volume, lost its bright color, and has the appearence of very well-cooked spinach—this step is integral to the success of this dish.

Return the cooked celery to the pan and fold into the meat and herb mixture as best you can. Add the lemon juice and a generous amount of salt and pepper and mix well. Then pour over enough boiling water to barely cover the ingredients. Cover the pan with a lid, reduce the heat to low, and cook for 1 hour, stirring occasionally.

Remove the lid and check and adjust the seasoning to taste, then cook, uncovered, for a further hour or so until the meat is tender before serving with plain basmati rice.

Spicy bulgur wheat meatballs
in garlicky tomato sauce

I once traveled to the Cappadocia region of Anatolia in central Turkey to visit the famous ancient rock formations. During that trip I fell in love with these tiny little meatballs containing bulgur wheat known as *sulu köfte*, and this is my homage to that dish. Traditionally, they are served as a soup or with a locally made pasta called *eriste*, but tagliatelle works beautifully.

SERVES 6 TO 8 (MAKES ABOUT 45 MEATBALLS)

1lb 2oz minced lamb (20% fat)

1¼ cups uncooked bulgur wheat

1 large onion, minced in a food
    processor or very finely chopped

1 tablespoon dried oregano

1 tablespoon garlic granules

1 teaspoon ground turmeric

1 teaspoon paprika

sea salt flakes and freshly ground
    black pepper

buttered tagliatelle, to serve

FOR THE SAUCE

3 to 4 tablespoons olive oil

1 large head of garlic, cloves separated
    and thinly sliced

2 x 14oz cans chopped tomatoes

2 cups cold water

½ to 1 teaspoon chile flakes, to taste

sea salt flakes and freshly ground
    black pepper

Put all the main ingredients into a large mixing bowl and, using your hands, work them together really well for a few minutes until evenly combined. Roll the mixture into 1½-inch balls, compressing the mixture firmly to ensure they retain their shape.

To make the sauce, place a large saucepan over medium heat and drizzle in the olive oil. Add the garlic and cook for a few minutes until translucent, without browning. Add the canned tomatoes, chile flakes, the water, and a generous amount of salt and pepper.

Bring the sauce to a gentle boil, add the meatballs, and stir to coat in the sauce. Partially cover with the lid and let simmer gently for about 1 hour or so until the meatballs are cooked through. You want to reduce the liquid to the consistency of a rich sauce, so remove the lid after 30 minutes if it looks too watery. Check and adjust the seasoning before serving with buttered tagliatelle.

SIMPLY DELICIOUS WITH...
Flame-roasted Bell Pepper, Pistachio & Dill Weed Yogurt (see page 42).

Naan-o-paneer-o-sabzi
Persian cheese platter

I know what you're thinking. A cheese platter? But if you want to know what Persians eat, from the banquets of royal palaces and lavish weddings down to the humblest of family meals, this dish is always there, all year round. Naan-o-paneer-o-sabzi (bread, cheese, herbs) we call it. It's the ubiquitous sharing plate served at the beginning of a meal but always on the table throughout. It really is stunningly simple and very useful to serve to guests to buy you some time in the kitchen if you are running a little behind with the cooking.

SERVES 4

16 radishes
8 scallions
generous handful of walnut halves
7oz block of vegetarian feta cheese
4 sprigs of tarragon
generous handful of mint leaves
generous handful of basil leaves
flatbread or tortilla wraps, quartered, to serve

Using a small sharp knife, cut a deep cross in the top of each radish running down close to the base, then plunge into a bowl of cold water. Trim the ends of the green parts of the scallions then trim the bulb end. Starting at the bulb end, cut a deep cross running halfway down the length of each scallion. Plunge into the bowl of cold water with the radishes. Let soak for about 1 hour.

Meanwhile, soak the walnuts for about 1 hour in hot water from the faucet.

Once the soaking time has elapsed, select a large wooden platter or cutting board and place the feta on it. Drain and rinse the walnuts, then drain them again and dry them. Drain the radishes and scallions and dry them, too.

Arrange the herbs, walnuts, radishes, and scallions on the platter or board. Serve with flatbread.

SIMPLY DELICIOUS WITH…
Kabab Koobideh (see page 82) or Tepsi Kebap (see page 84).

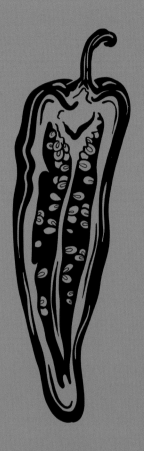

The melting pot

Zucchini & oregano pancakes
with feta & honey

Zucchini are so versatile, and I absolutely love the Turkish take on them in the form of zucchini and feta fritters, known as *mücver*. Taking inspiration from them, these pancakes make a wonderful breakfast or brunch dish, topped with creamy, salty feta, and a good drizzle of sweet honey. They are my idea of perfection.

MAKES ABOUT 16

2 large zucchini

2 eggs

¼ cup all-purpose flour

1 teaspoon baking powder

½ small pack (about ½oz) of oregano, leaves finely chopped

1 teaspoon cumin seeds

1 heaped teaspoon pul biber chile flakes, plus extra to serve

vegetable oil, for frying

sea salt flakes and freshly ground black pepper

TO SERVE

3½oz vegetarian feta cheese, crumbled

liquid honey

Coarsely grate the zucchini into a bowl. Tip the gratings into a clean dish towel, gather up the sides, and squeeze out the liquid. Place in a mixing bowl, add the eggs, flour, baking powder, oregano, cumin, and pul biber. Season generously with salt and pepper and beat together.

Place a large skillet over medium-high heat and drizzle in some vegetable oil. Using a tablespoon measure, roughly fill the scoop with the zucchini mixture and, without overcrowding, add dollops to the skillet, then lightly flatten. Fry for about 1 minute until the undersides are nicely browned, then flip them over and cook until the other sides have browned. Remove from the pan and repeat with the remaining mixture.

Serve the pancakes immediately topped with the crumbled feta, a little drizzle of honey, and a sprinkling of pul biber.

SIMPLY DELICIOUS WITH...
Roasted Nectarines with Labneh, Herbs & Honey (see page 69).

Harissa chicken noodle lettuce cups

Lettuce cups are one of my favorite things to eat. I'll pile them high with flavorful fillings and munch on them at any opportunity. This combo of sweet and spicy noodles with shredded chicken is a great one for sharing and especially perfect in the warmer months (I never let a thing like weather dictate when I eat these). They're a perfectly virtuous snack, finger food, or main meal.

SERVES 4 TO 6

2 boneless, skinless chicken breasts

2½oz rice vermicelli noodles, cooked following the package directions and rinsed until cold

2½oz fine green beans, thinly sliced

4 scallions, thinly sliced from root to tip

1 carrot, peeled, cut lengthwise into thirds, and then into matchsticks

1 small pack (about 1oz) of fresh cilantro, finely chopped

3 heads of Baby Romaine lettuce, leaves carefully separated

sea salt flakes and freshly ground black pepper

FOR THE DRESSING

2 tablespoons liquid honey

1 heaped tablespoon rose harissa

1 tablespoon soy sauce

1 tablespoon olive oil

finely grated zest and juice of 1 lime

1 heaped teaspoon nigella seeds

sea salt flakes

Bring a saucepan of water to a gentle boil, add the chicken breasts, and poach for 8 to 10 minutes, or until the juices run clear when the thickest part of the meat is pierced with the tip of a sharp knife.

Remove the chicken with a slotted spoon and let cool. Shred the meat and then coarsely chop.

Mix all the dressing ingredients together in a measuring cup or small bowl.

Reserve 2 tablespoons of the dressing, then add everything, except the lettuce, to a mixing bowl. Season with salt and pepper and mix together well.

Arrange the lettuce leaves on a serving platter. Divide the chicken noodle mixture among the lettuce leaves and serve drizzled with the reserved dressing.

SIMPLY DELICIOUS WITH...

Tomato & Peanut Salad with Tamarind, Ginger & Honey Dressing (see page 137) or Crispy Shrimp with Mango & Tomato Dip (see page 164).

Harissa & lime chicken wings

Sweet, spicy, citrusy, barbecued, Asian—you name it, I have love for all chicken wing recipes. I know what you're thinking looking at the ingredients below ("fish sauce?!") But trust me, this is inspired by Thai fish sauce chicken wings, which are crispy, salty, and incredibly delicious. Of course, I have come up with my own version, which is the kind of comforting, finger-lickin' food that should really be made in double portions.

SERVES 4 TO 6

vegetable oil, for deep-frying
2¼lb chicken wings

FOR THE SAUCE
3 tablespoons fish sauce
3 tablespoons liquid honey
2 tablespoons rose harissa
finely grated zest of 1 lime and
    juice of ½

Mix all the sauce ingredients together in a large mixing bowl and set aside.

Pour enough oil into a saucepan or deep skillet to fill to a depth of about 3 inches. Heat the oil over medium-high heat and bring to frying temperature (about 410°F). Carefully dip a chicken wing into the oil. If it sizzles immediately, the oil is hot enough, but if it bubbles ferociously, then the oil is too hot, so reduce the heat before you begin cooking. Line a plate with a double layer of paper towels.

When the oil is ready for frying, carefully add the chicken wings to the oil and stir briefly to stop them from sticking to one another. Deep-fry the chicken for 20 to 25 minutes, or until crispy and golden brown and cooked through (you may need to do this in 2 batches). Remove the chicken from the oil with a slotted spoon and transfer to the lined plate to drain. Keep the first batch warm under foil while you cook the second batch.

While still hot, add the chicken wings to the sauce and toss until well coated, then serve immediately.

SIMPLY DELICIOUS WITH...
Baked Sweet Potato Fries with Za'atar & Garlic (see page 34).

Lamb, cumin, cilantro & chile kebabs

My local Pakistani restaurant has always made the most insanely delicious lamb kebabs, and while this recipe is very different, it is inspired by their fiery and aromatic creation, and simplified to suit home cooking using a ridged grill pan on the stove. These are a delicious delight and perfect with a little cooling yogurt on the side.

MAKES 6

1lb 2oz ground lamb (20% fat)

1 onion, minced in a food processor and drained of any liquid, or very finely chopped

4 fat garlic cloves, minced

1¼ cups fresh cilantro, finely chopped

1 tablespoon cumin seeds

1 to 2 teaspoons chile flakes, to taste

sea salt flakes and freshly ground black pepper

pul biber chile flakes, to garnish

TO SERVE

rice or flatbread

Greek or plain yogurt

Put all the main ingredients into a large mixing bowl and, using your hands, work them together really well, pummeling the meat mixture for several minutes into a smooth paste.

Divide the mixture into 6 portions and form each portion into a sausage shape, then thread onto 6 metal or wooden skewers. Roll each sausage on a smooth cutting board to elongate to about 4½ inches in length.

Preheat a nonstick ridged grill pan over high heat. Once hot, cook the kebabs for 8 to 10 minutes, turning them halfway through the cooking time, until nicely browned on both sides and cooked through.

Sprinkle with pul biber and serve with rice or flatbread and Greek or plain yogurt.

SIMPLY DELICIOUS WITH...

Butternut Borani (see page 75) or Naan-o-Paneer-o-Sabzi (see page 108).

TIP
Alternatively, cook these kebabs in the oven at its highest setting for 12 minutes, or until cooked through and just starting to brown.

Spiced lamb, date, pine nut & feta melts

Initially, I made this filling for pastry cigars at a cookery class of mine a few years back. There was a little left over, so I took it home to make a quick supper for myself, and I actually preferred this way of using the mixture. It's really quite indulgent, but again very simple. The sweet, spiced meat mixture works beautifully with the creamy, salty feta and satisfies on every level.

MAKES 8

2 tablespoons vegetable oil

1 large onion, minced in a food
  processor or very finely chopped

1lb 2oz ground lamb (20% fat)

3 heaped teaspoons ground cinnamon

2 heaped teaspoons garlic granules

½ teaspoon cayenne pepper

1 cup pitted, finely chopped dates

1 small pack (about 1oz) of flat leaf
  parsley, very finely chopped

juice of ¼ lemon

½ cup pine nuts

3 tablespoons liquid honey

8 mini flour tortilla wraps

2 x 7oz blocks of feta cheese, crumbled

1 teaspoon pul biber chile flakes

sea salt flakes and freshly ground
  black pepper

Place a large skillet over medium-high heat and drizzle in the vegetable oil. Add the onion and cook for a few minutes until soft and golden. Add the ground lamb and immediately begin breaking the meat up as finely as you can to avoid clumps. Turn the heat up to high, add the cinnamon, garlic granules, cayenne, and a generous amount of pepper and stir until the meat is well coated in the spices. Continue cooking until the meat is fully cooked.

Remove the pan from the heat and stir in the dates, parsley, lemon juice, pine nuts, and honey, then season the mixture with a generous amount of salt, mix well, and set aside to cool completely.

Preheat your broiler or oven to its highest setting. Line a large baking pan with nonstick parchment paper and arrange the wraps on the pan (you may need to do this in 2 batches). Divide the lamb mixture into 8 equal portions and spread a portion onto each wrap. Scatter each generously with crumbled feta and place under the broiler or in the oven for 6 to 7 minutes until the cheese browns. Sprinkle the pul biber on top and serve.

SIMPLY DELICIOUS WITH...

Fennel Salad with Spinach, Cashew & Coriander Seed Dressing (see page 53).

Harissa kofta lettuce cups
with preserved lemon yogurt

These spicy North African-inspired koftas are absolutely addictive, and paired with the citrus yet cooling yogurt, it does become somewhat impossible to limit yourself to a sensible number. Personally, I like to eat a few as they come, but when I'm really hungry, I will toast and split open a pitta bread and shove a few of the koftas inside for a deeply satisfying snack or meal.

MAKES 10 CUPS

1lb 2oz ground lamb (20% fat)

3 tablespoons rose harissa

2 large eggs

1 large onion, minced in a food
    processor and any liquid drained,
    or very finely chopped

½ cup very finely chopped fresh
    flat leaf parsley

½ cup very finely chopped fresh
    cilantro

2 teaspoons ground coriander

2 teaspoons garlic granules

2 teaspoons ground cinnamon

½ cup pine nuts

vegetable oil

generous amount of sea salt flakes and
    freshly ground black pepper

FOR THE PRESERVED
LEMON YOGURT

2 cups Greek yogurt

2 teaspoons dried oregano

1 small pack (about 1oz) of mint,
    leaves stacked, rolled up together,
    and finely sliced widthwise into
    thin ribbons

5 to 6 small preserved lemons, seeded
    and very finely chopped

generous drizzle of olive oil

generous amount of sea salt flakes and
    freshly ground black pepper

TO SERVE

about 3 heads of Baby Romaine
    lettuce, leaves carefully separated

3 scallions, very thinly sliced
    diagonally from root to tip

1 to 2 teaspoons pul biber chile flakes,
    to taste

CONTINUED OVERLEAF

Mix all the preserved lemon yogurt ingredients together in a small bowl, then set aside.

Put all the main ingredients, except the vegetable oil, into a large mixing bowl and, using your hands, work them together really well, pummeling the meat mixture for several minutes into a smooth paste.

Take golf-ball-sized amounts of the mixture, roll into balls, and then elongate into kofta shapes. Make about 20 in total.

Heat a large skillet over medium heat. Once hot, drizzle in a little of the vegetable oil and fry the koftas in batches for 4 to 5 minutes on each side until they are nicely browned and cooked through on both sides. Use a spatula to scrape them out of the pan.

Fill as many lettuce leaf "cups" as you need generously with the preserved lemon yogurt, then add a kofta or two to each cup, dollop with a little more yogurt, and top with the scallions and a sprinkle of pul biber.

SIMPLY DELICIOUS WITH...

Smoked Eggplant, Tomato, Tamarind, & Peanut Salad (see page 182) or Watermelon, Black Olive & Feta with Cayenne, Honey & Lime Dressing (see page 143).

Polow-e-bademjan-o-felfel

This fried eggplant, bell pepper, and tomato rice isn't a classic Persian dish, but it is very good, and I've made it vegan friendly by using oil instead of butter to ensure no one is left out. I've added sweet red bell peppers to round this dish off and make it a proper meal, which means there is not much else you need on the side, except maybe a dollop of yogurt or a nice spicy pickle relish or chutney.

SERVES 6 TO 8

vegetable oil, for frying

3 large eggplant, peeled and cut into
    1½-inch cubes

2 large onions, coarsely chopped

2 red bell peppers, cored, seeded,
    and diced

1 teaspoon chile flakes

1 teaspoon black mustard seeds

1 teaspoon cumin seeds

1 teaspoon ground turmeric

3 tablespoons tomato paste

2½ cups basmati rice

sea salt flakes and freshly ground
    black pepper

Line a large platter with a double layer of paper towels. Place a large saucepan over high heat and pour in enough vegetable oil to fill to a depth of about 1 inch. Once hot, add the eggplant cubes and stir until well coated in the oil. Cook for about 15 minutes until browned, stirring only occasionally. Remove with a slotted spoon, shaking off any excess oil, then transfer to the lined platter to drain.

Pour off most of the oil in the pan, then return to a medium-high heat. Add the onions and cook them for a few minutes until softened and translucent. Then add the red bell peppers and cook until softened (but not browned). Next, add the chile flakes, mustard seeds, cumin seeds, turmeric, and tomato paste and stir-fry for 3 to 4 minutes.

Tip the vegetable mixture into a large mixing bowl, add the eggplant cubes, and season with a very generous amount of salt and pepper (as the mixture will need the extra seasoning once combined with the rice).

Bring a large, ideally nonstick, saucepan of water to a boil. Add the rice and stir to stop the grains from sticking together. Parboil for about 6 to 7 minutes until the grains turn from a dullish off-white color to a more opaque, brilliant white and have slightly elongated.

CONTINUED OVERLEAF

Drain and immediately rinse thoroughly under cold running water, running your fingers through the rice, until all the grains are well rinsed of starch and completely cooled. Drain the rice thoroughly by shaking the sieve well, then let stand over the sink for 5 to 10 minutes to allow any remaining water to drain away. Shake off any excess water before use.

Rinse the rice saucepan and place over very low heat heat. If the pan isn't nonstick, first line the bottom with a large square of nonstick parchment paper (see Tip on page 102). Add ¼ cup vegetable oil, then pour in enough cold water to come ½ inch up the inside of the pan. Swirl the pan around to mix the oil and water together, then add a generous amount of crushed salt flakes. Loosely scatter just enough of the rice into the pan to coat the bottom in an even layer (don't pack the mixture into the pan), then mix the rest of the rice with the vegetable mixture until evenly combined. Scatter (do not press) the rice mixture into the pan, allowing for natural air pockets, and smooth it out to the sides. Using the handle of a wooden spoon, poke a series of holes into the rice, piercing all the way to the bottom of the pan (this allows the steam to circulate). Wrap the pan lid in a clean dish cloth so that it fits tightly on the pan. If using a gas stove, cook over the lowest flame for 1 hour, but if using an electric/induction stove, cook over medium heat for 20 minutes, then reduce the heat to medium-low and cook for a further 1½ to 2 hours.

Once cooked, remove the lid and smooth the rice over to the edges to level it off. Place a large platter over the pan. Carefully invert the polow onto the platter to reveal the crunchy *tahdig* crust.

SIMPLY DELICIOUS WITH...

Lamb, Cumin, Coriander & Chile Kebabs (see page 118) and Pomegranate Molasses & Honey-glazed Meatballs (see page 56).

Steak tartines *with tarragon & paprika butter*

The only slight problem with these little tartines is that they are impossible to eat gracefully. You can make mini versions to serve to your guests as canapés. Either way, they are a winner.

MAKES 4

vegetable oil, for frying

1 large red onion, halved and cut into
    half moons ¼-inch in thickness

1 teaspoon fennel seeds

1½ cups drained sun-dried tomatoes
    packed in oil

½ cup Greek yogurt

1 to 2 teaspoons water, if needed

2 x 7oz sirloin steaks

4 large slices of sourdough, toasted

sea salt flakes and black pepper

**FOR THE TARRAGON
& PAPRIKA BUTTER**

3½ tablespoons butter, at room
    temperature

2 garlic cloves, minced

1 heaped teaspoon paprika

½ small pack (about ½oz) of tarragon,
    leaves very finely chopped, plus
    4 to 8 leaves to garnish (optional)

Place a large skillet over medium-high heat and drizzle in a little vegetable oil. Add the onion and fennel seeds and stir until well coated in the oil. Cook for 6 to 8 minutes until slightly charred in places, stirring occasionally. Remove from the pan and transfer to a plate.

Beat the soft butter with the garlic, paprika, and tarragon in a small bowl, then season with a generous amount of salt and pepper. Set aside.

Put the sun-dried tomatoes into a bowl, reserving 4 to 8 pieces to garnish. Add the yogurt. Use a hand-held stick blender to blitz until combined and smooth, adding the water if necessary.

Return the skillet to high heat. Rub the steaks with a little vegetable oil and season on both sides with a very generous amount of pepper to form a thin pepper crust. Once the pan is very hot, place the steaks in the pan (they should sizzle) and cook for about 2 to 3 minutes on each side until they are nicely charred. Remove the steaks from the pan, transfer to a plate, and let rest for 10 minutes.

Using a sharp knife, very thinly slice the steak. Place a small saucepan over medium heat, add the tarragon and paprika butter and, once melted, toss in the steak strips. Remove the pan from the heat and set aside.

Spread the tomato yogurt generously over the toasted bread. Divide the steak among the slices of toast, top with the onion and then with tomato and tarragon, if liked. Serve immediately.

Lazy beef & caramelized onion pide

I love Turkish *pide* and Georgian *hachapuri*, but you really need time and patience to make the dough from scratch. This is a quicker, lighter version using puff pastry to satisfy my inner lazy girl. It's perfect for sharing, but only if you're in a sharing mood, of course.

MAKES 4

vegetable oil, for frying

2 red onions, halved and very thinly
    sliced into half moons

1lb 2oz ground beef

1 teaspoon cumin seeds

1 teaspoon ground cinnamon

1 teaspoon chile flakes

1 teaspoon ground turmeric

2 tablespoons tomato paste

1 red bell pepper, cored, seeded,
    and finely diced

1 small pack (about 1oz) of dill weed,
    finely chopped

1 small pack (about 1oz) of flat leaf
    parsley, finely chopped

⅓ cup pine nuts

2 x 11oz ready-rolled all-butter puff
    pastry sheets

sea salt flakes and freshly ground
    black pepper

Preheat the oven to 400°F.

Place a skillet over medium heat, drizzle in a little oil, and fry the onions for 25 to 30 minutes until very soft and caramelized, stirring occasionally to stop them from browning too much.

Add the ground beef to the skillet and break it up as finely as you can to avoid clumps. While it's still uncooked, add the cumin seeds, cinnamon, chile flakes, turmeric, and tomato paste. Mix well into the meat, then continue cooking the meat until it is well browned. Add the red bell pepper and stir-fry until softened. Season generously with salt and pepper, then remove the skillet from the heat and stir through the herbs and pine nuts. Set aside.

Cut each pastry sheet in half lengthwise to make 4 long rectangles, then lay these onto baking pans. Divide the meat mixture between the pastry rectangles, leaving a generous border of pastry around the edges. Using your index finger and thumb, make small twists in the pastry edges to form slightly raised crimps. Taper either end of each pastry into a point to form a boat shape. Bake for about 25 to 30 minutes, or until the pastry is a deep golden brown. Serve immediately.

SIMPLY DELICIOUS WITH...

Carrot, Pistachio & Dill Weed Salad with Lime & Honey Dressing (see page 51).

Lamb, tomato & barley soup

Soups, or *aash* as we call them in Persian, are a staple of the nation. They are far heartier than most other soups and while this isn't a traditional recipe, using barley certainly is. Think of this less as a soup and more as a comforting one-pot meal.

SERVES 8

1¾lb lamb neck fillets cut into
　½-inch cubes
½ cup all-purpose flour
¾ stick butter
2 large white onions, finely chopped
4 fat garlic cloves, thinly sliced
¼ cup tomato paste
olive oil, for frying
1 tablespoon dried mint
5 large tomatoes, coarsely diced
1 quart lamb or vegetable stock

1 quart cold water
finely grated zest and juice of
　1 lemon
½ cup pearl barley
1 small pack (about 1oz) of chives,
　finely snipped
sea salt flakes and freshly ground
　black pepper
sour cream, to serve (optional)

Heat a large saucepan over medium heat. Meanwhile, dust the lamb cubes with the flour, shaking off any excess. Add the butter to the pan, and once melted, brown the lamb on all sides.

Add the onions, garlic, tomato paste, and a little olive oil to the pan, mix well, and let fry for a few minutes. Then add the dried mint and tomatoes and stir until coated in the onion mixture.

Pour in the stock and cold water and add the lemon zest and juice and a generous amount of salt and pepper. Bring the contents of the pan to a rolling boil, then reduce the heat to low, and partially cover the pan with a lid. Let this simmer gently for 1 hour, stirring occasionally. Check the liquid level of the soup and top it off a little with water if the broth has reduced too much (once you add the barley it will absorb some of the liquid).

Partially cover the pan with the lid as before and simmer the soup for a further 30 minutes before adding the barley, stirring well as it goes in. Cook, uncovered, for another 45 minutes or until the barley is cooked, then taste and adjust the seasoning if necessary.

Remove the pan from the heat, and stir in the chives just before serving (saving some for a garnish). Dollop a little sour cream on top with the reserved chives to serve, if liked.

Chilled cucumber & pistachio soup

Inspired by the Spanish chilled almond soup ajo blanco, I came up with a Persian variation that not only utilizes our most revered nut, but adds cucumber to dilute the creaminess a little and make it the perfect light refreshment all year round. Back in my catering days, I would serve it in shot glasses as an interesting canapé or pre-appetizer, or middle course. It really is fantastic stuff and even better with some nice crusty bread on the side.

SERVES 4

¾ cup pistachio slivers (or very coarsely chopped whole nuts), plus extra to garnish

1 small onion, peeled and quartered

1 large cucumber, peeled and coarsely chopped

1 small pack (about 1oz) of dill weed, coarsely chopped, reserving 4 sprigs, to garnish

1 small pack (about 1oz) of mint, leaves picked

2 garlic cloves, coarsely chopped

1 small slice of crusty bread, coarsely chopped

1 tablespoon vegan red wine vinegar

1 cup cold water

sea salt flakes and freshly ground black pepper

olive oil, for drizzling

Put the pistachios, onion, cucumber, herbs, garlic, bread, and vinegar into a blender and blitz until smooth.

Season to taste with salt and pepper, then add the cold water and briefly blend to combine and to thin the puree to a soup consistency. Serve immediately, drizzled with olive oil. Scatter with extra pistachio slivers and add a dill weed sprig to garnish.

SIMPLY DELICIOUS WITH...

Strawberry, Soft Goat Cheese & Pistachio Salad (see page 179) or Harissa Kofta Lettuce Cups with Preserved Lemon Yogurt (see page 123).

Tomato & peanut salad
with tamarind, ginger & honey dressing

I find myself turning to tamarind as a flavor base more and more these days. It offers the acidity of both lemons and vinegar, but is not remotely as overpowering as either of those ingredients. In fact, pair it with something sweet such as honey, and you still get the acidity but in a wonderfully gentle and well rounded capacity. Here, it makes the perfect dressing for this simple salad of tomatoes, and the ginger adds another flavor dimension that makes it impossible not to keep eating this salad until it's all gone.

SERVES 4 TO 6

1 small red onion, minced

7oz baby plum tomatoes, halved

2 handfuls of salted peanuts

1 small pack (about 1oz) of fresh
cilantro, coarsely chopped

FOR THE DRESSING

3-inch piece of fresh ginger root,
peeled and finely grated

2 tablespoons olive oil

1 heaped tablespoon unsweetened
tamarind paste

1 tablespoon light soy sauce

1 tablespoon liquid honey

small amount of sea salt flakes

freshly ground black pepper

Mix all the dressing ingredients together in a small bowl. Add the onion and let soak for about 20 minutes to soften.

Add the tomatoes, peanuts, and cilantro to a bowl. Pour the onion and dressing mixture over them, and stir to combine. Serve the salad at room temperature.

SIMPLY DELICIOUS WITH...

Chorizo, Goat Cheese & Cumin Borek (see page 148) or Goat Cheese, Vegetable & Za'atar Filo Tart (see page 207).

TIP
Substitute agave syrup or superfine sugar for the honey to make this recipe suitable for vegans.

Corn, black bean & avocado salad

Corn reminds me of my childhood, when I usually ate straight from the can. As an adult, I prefer to cook whole cobs and enjoy the rich, intense sweetness of the kernels. A good corn salad can be the perfect pairing with so many ingredients, but my travels to Thailand have inspired the addition of Thai lime leaves for a flavor like no other. This is a spicy salad, which, of course, you can tame by using fewer chiles. However, I've served this to people who aren't chile lovers and they enjoyed it so much I decided to share the recipe here with you.

SERVES 10 TO 12

6 cobs of corn, silk and husk removed

2 avocados, peeled, stoned, and diced

14oz can black beans, drained and rinsed

4 Thai lime leaves, very finely chopped

4 scallions, thinly sliced

1 small red bell pepper, cored, seeded, and finely diced

1 small green bell pepper, cored, seeded, and finely diced

2 long red chiles, seeded and minced

1 small pack (about 1oz) of fresh cilantro, finely chopped

2 heaped tablespoons mayonnaise

drizzle of olive oil

sea salt flakes and freshly ground black pepper

Cook the cobs of corn in a saucepan of boiling water for about 10 minutes until tender. Drain and rinse under cold running water until cool, then drain again.

Hold each cob in turn upright on a cutting board. Then, using a sharp knife, cut from the top to the bottom to slice off the kernels in strips.

Add the kernels to a bowl with all the remaining ingredients and mix together well. Season to taste with salt and pepper and serve.

SIMPLY DELICIOUS WITH...

Harissa & Lime Chicken Wings (see page 116) or Spiced Pork Wraps with Green Apple Salsa (see page 167).

TIP

This is a large salad, so halve the ingredients to make a smaller batch.

Chargrilled eggplant
with red bell pepper, chile & walnut sauce

I often say that the eggplant is the meat of the Middle East. Here I pair them with a romesco-inspired sauce, which seasons the eggplant beautifully. Leftovers, as standard, should be piled into some crusty bread with feta cheese. This is my best advice to you, and you may just thank me for it.

SERVES 6 TO 8

2 large or 3 small eggplant, cut into disks ½ inch in thickness

garlic oil, for brushing

generous handful of green olives, pitted

1 small pack (about 1oz) of flat leaf parsley, coarsely chopped

sea salt flakes and freshly ground black pepper

FOR THE SAUCE

1 red bell pepper, cored, seeded, and coarsely chopped

1 long red chile, coarsely chopped

½ cup walnut pieces, plus extra to garnish (optional)

1 fat garlic clove, peeled

1 tablespoon red wine vinegar

olive oil

Put all the ingredients for the sauce into a blender with 3 tablespoons of olive oil and blitz until smooth. Season to taste with salt and pepper and set aside.

Heat a ridged grill pan over medium-high heat. Using a pastry brush, brush one side of the eggplant slices with just enough garlic oil to coat the surface. Once the pan is hot, working in batches, add the eggplant slices, oiled-side down, and chargrill for about 6 to 8 minutes, then brush the top sides with garlic oil before you turn them over and cook for a further 6 to 8 minutes until nicely charred and cooked through. Remove from the pan and let cool. Repeat with the remaining slices.

Arrange the charred slices on a large platter and season with salt and pepper. Pour the sauce liberally over them and top with the olives and parsley. Scatter with some extra walnuts to garnish, if liked, and drizzle with a little olive oil before serving.

SIMPLY DELICIOUS WITH...

Marinated Steak with Labneh, Pul Biber Butter & Crispy Onions (see page 188) or Lamb, Cumin, Coriander & Chile Kebabs (see page 118).

Watermelon, black olive & feta
with cayenne, honey & lime dressing

Feta and watermelon are a typical Eastern pairing, and when I was looking for a recipe using them, I spotted frozen feta on the Instagram of James Cochran, a chef friend of mine, so I borrowed this little trick from him. Freezing the feta enables you to grate it, which means the flavor you get is rather more subtle in its saltiness than you would achieve using chunks of feta. The dressing is really what brings this dish together. Sweet and citrusy, it makes it such a great salad for the summer.

SERVES 4 TO 6

about 2¼lb watermelon, quartered, seeded, and very thinly sliced (like carpaccio)

finely grated zest of 1 fat lime

½oz chervil (see Tip), leaves coarsely chopped

generous handful of Greek basil leaves

2 handfuls of pitted Kalamata olives

3½oz vegetarian feta cheese, frozen

handful of pistachio slivers (or very coarsely chopped whole nuts)

freshly ground black pepper

FOR THE DRESSING

2 tablespoons liquid honey

½ teaspoon cayenne pepper

2 tablespoons olive oil

juice of the lime zested above

generous amount of sea salt flakes

Arrange the watermelon slices on a large platter, season well with pepper, and scatter with the lime zest.

Mix the dressing ingredients together in a small bowl, then drizzle it all over the watermelon slices. Then scatter the slices with the fresh herbs and olives. Remove the frozen feta from the freezer and finely grate it over the watermelon. Scatter with the pistachios and serve immediately.

SIMPLY DELICIOUS WITH...

Harissa Chicken Noodle Lettuce Cups (see page 115) or Harissa & Lime Chicken Wings (see page 116).

TIP

If you can't find fresh chervil, use fresh mint leaves instead.

Ghayour house chicken kari

Admittedly, this isn't exactly a Persian classic, but every time I make this I am asked for the recipe. So, here it is! I hope, like me, you find it to be a very useful, straightforward curry base. You can substitute the chicken with shrimp, or use vegetables such as cauliflower, squash, zucchini, or root vegetables to make a vegetarian or vegan alternative.

SERVES 4 TO 6

¼ cup vegetable oil

1 teaspoon black mustard seeds

1 teaspoon fenugreek seeds

1 teaspoon cumin seeds

1 teaspoon coriander seeds

1 cassia bark stick (not a cinnamon stick, as they are too strong)

3 cardamom pods, crushed

1 large onion, very finely chopped

3-inch piece of fresh ginger root, peeled and grated or very finely chopped

4 fat garlic cloves, bashed and thinly sliced

1 to 2 small green hot chiles or 1 to 2 large long red chiles to taste, stalks intact and split

8 large bone-in, skinless chicken thighs

2 teaspoons ground turmeric

4 large tomatoes, coarsely diced

14oz can chopped tomatoes

sea salt flakes and freshly ground black pepper

flatbread or steamed rice, to serve

Place a large saucepan over medium-high heat and pour in the vegetable oil. Add the mustard, fenugreek, cumin and coriander seeds, the cassia bark, and the cardamom pods and fry, shaking the pan, until the mustard seeds begin to pop. Stir in the onion and let fry for a few minutes more until it begins to brown and caramelize but without burning.

Add the ginger, garlic, and chiles to the pan and briefly stir-fry for a minute or so, then add the chicken thighs, turmeric, and a generous amount of salt and pepper. Stir the mixture until the chicken is well coated in the onion and spice mixture. Add the fresh tomatoes followed by the canned tomatoes, then add just enough cold water to cover the chicken. Reduce the heat and let simmer gently for 2 hours, stirring occasionally to prevent it from sticking to the pan. Top off the liquid level with a little cold water if necessary.

Fish out and discard the cassia bark and cardamom pods, then check and adjust the seasoning before serving with flatbread or steamed rice.

SIMPLY DELICIOUS WITH...

Adas Polow (see page 101).

Sticky harissa, sesame & pistachio chicken

This recipe embodies all the qualities (sticky, savory, spicy, crunchy, and utterly delicious) I like in a chicken dish. It reminds me of Cantonese sticky chicken dishes, but with a little more oomph and, more importantly, it can be easily recreated at home.

SERVES 3 TO 4

1lb 2oz boneless, skinless
    chicken breasts

vegetable oil, for frying

1 teaspoon ground cinnamon

1 teaspoon garlic granules

3 tablespoons liquid honey

2 tablespoons rose harissa

2½ tablespoons sesame seeds, toasted

½ cup pistachio nuts, coarsely
    chopped

sea salt flakes and freshly ground
    black pepper

Lay the chicken breasts flat on a cutting board and coarsely chop into fillets.

Heat a large skillet over high heat and drizzle in a little vegetable oil. Once hot, add the chicken strips and quickly toss in the oil. Sear the chicken on the outside until opaque all over but not cooked through.

Add the cinnamon and garlic granules and quickly toss the chicken in them, then add the honey and harissa and stir until the chicken is well coated. Season with a generous amount of salt and pepper. Let the chicken fry for about 1 minute until cooked through, then stir to coat in the sauce.

Once the sauce is bubbling and reduced to a consistency almost like caramel, remove the pan from the heat. Stir and then sprinkle it with the toasted sesame seeds and the pistachios to serve.

SIMPLY DELICIOUS WITH...

Carrot, Pistachio & Dill Weed Salad with Lime & Honey Dressing (see page 51) or Tomato & Peanut Salad with Tamarind, Ginger & Honey Dressing (see page 137).

TIP
You can also use chicken tenders for this recipe.

Chorizo, goats' cheese & cumin borek

Although not a traditional borek filling, this wonderful combination of smoky, spiced chorizo and cumin-spiked, creamy goat cheese is a winner. Chorizo really is such a fantastic ingredient and its ability to deliver loads of flavor to anything it comes into contact with always makes it a crowd-pleaser and a refrigerator staple in my household.

SERVES 4 TO 6

2 x 7oz cured (not cooking) chorizo sausages, skinned and cut into chunks

2 teaspoons cumin seeds, toasted

12oz rindless soft goat cheese

vegetable oil, for oiling

6 sheets of filo pastry (each about 19 x 10 inches)

1 tablespoon milk or water

beaten egg, to glaze

1 teaspoon nigella seeds

Preheat the oven to 400°F.

Put the chunks of chorizo into a food processor and process until they are ground as finely as possible. Transfer to a mixing bowl, add the cumin seeds and goat cheese, and stir together to combine evenly.

Brush the bottom of a 10-inch round pie plate or cake pan with a little vegetable oil. Lay a pastry sheet in it lengthwise with the ends overhanging the sides. Then lay another pastry sheet on top in the same way, but widthwise. Divide the chorizo filling in half and place one half onto the filo in the plate or pan, smoothing it right to the edges to cover the bottom evenly. Fold another pastry sheet in half to create a double thickness and lay it over the filling, then repeat with a second pastry sheet to form a thick pastry layer. Brush the pastry with the milk or water, then top with the remaining filling, pushing and patting it into place to evenly coat the pastry layer. Fold the overhanging pastry into the center, then gently crumple up the remaining 2 pastry sheets and arrange on top.

Brush all the exposed pastry and edges with beaten egg and sprinkle with the nigella seeds. Bake for 25 to 30 minutes until deep golden brown. Serve immediately.

SIMPLY DELICIOUS WITH...

Pear, Chickpea & Green Leaf Salad with Maple Harissa Dressing (see page 172).

Silk Road-style lamb & cumin pasta

I know this sounds like a weird combination to be thrown over pasta, and I realize it may seem like it's kind of heavy on the cumin (which it is). But it really works, and I have won over quite a few skeptics with this recipe. This is mostly because it's actually—and perhaps for some surprisingly—very delicious and satisfying. Try it! It's one of my favorite recipes in this book and I knew instantly that I had to share it with you.

SERVES 4

1lb 2oz lamb leg steaks or other lamb steaks

1 tablespoon garlic granules

2 tablespoons cumin seeds, toasted and ground (see Tip on page 15)

1 tablespoon chile flakes

1 teaspoon ground cinnamon

1 teaspoon ground coriander

3 tablespoons olive oil

1 teaspoon toasted sesame oil

¼ cup light soy sauce, or more to taste

1 teaspoon rice vinegar

9oz tagliatelle

3½ tablespoons butter

sea salt flakes and freshly ground black pepper

Place the lamb steaks between 2 layers of plastic wrap and bash the meat with a meat tenderizer or a rolling pin to flatten and tenderize the meat. Discard the plastic wrap and thinly slice the lamb into strips about ¼ inch in thickness. Place the lamb strips in a nonmetallic bowl, add the garlic granules, spices, oils, soy sauce, vinegar, and a generous amount of salt and pepper and mix together well. Cover the bowl with plastic wrap and let marinate at room temperature for at least 1 hour.

Cook the tagliatelle in a large saucepan of salted boiling water following the package directions, then drain the pasta, reserving the pasta cooking water.

Meanwhile, heat a wok or large skillet over high heat. Once hot, add the lamb along with the marinade and cook for a few minutes until seared all over, but avoid stirring constantly. Remove the pan from the heat to ensure the meat stays slightly rare and tender. Add the butter and season to taste with salt, pepper, or soy sauce. Add the cooked pasta together with 2 to 3 ladles of the reserved pasta water. Mix well using tongs, adding more of the cooking water to the pasta to loosen, if liked. Serve immediately, no accompaniment needed.

Fragrant fish cakes
with preserved lemon mayonnaise

Many Brits avoid dill weed with white fish (especially those who grew up in the 1980s eating vacuum-packed white fish in dill weed sauce), but it still remains one of my favorite pairings. The preserved lemon mayo provides a hit of salty citrus that works incredibly with the fish cake.

MAKES 6 TO 8

FOR THE FISH CAKES
vegetable oil, for frying
10½oz skinless chunky white fish
    fillet, such as cod, hake, or
    haddock, diced
2 cups mashed potatoes
1 small pack (about 1oz) of dill weed,
    finely chopped
1 small pack (about 1oz) of fresh
    cilantro, finely chopped
2 tablespoons powdered mustard
¼ cup all-purpose flour

1 teaspoon chile flakes
1 teaspoon ground ginger
1 teaspoon garlic granules
1 egg
sea salt flakes and freshly ground
    black pepper

FOR THE PRESERVED LEMON
MAYONNAISE
3 small preserved lemons, seeded and finely
    chopped
heaped ¼ cup mayonnaise

Place a skillet over very low heat, drizzle in a tiny amount of oil, and add the fish. Cook for 6 to 8 minutes until just opaque. Transfer the fish to a sieve, break into flakes, and let drain.

Preheat your oven to its highest setting.

Put the fish with all the remaining fish-cake ingredients into a mixing bowl and season well with salt and pepper. Using your hands, work the ingredients together really well, pummeling the mixture for several minutes into a smooth, even paste (the more you work the mixture, the better it will bind together). Shape into 6 to 8 patties. Place the patties on a nonstick baking pan and bake for 12 minutes until just starting to brown. Remove from the oven and finish cooking the fish cakes in a hot skillet with a drizzle of oil for 4 to 6 minutes on each side, or until nicely browned.

Mix the preserved lemons with the mayonnaise in a small bowl, season with pepper, and serve with the hot fish cakes.

SIMPLY DELICIOUS WITH...
Green Bean Salad with Tahini, Preserved Lemon & Pine Nuts (see page 47).

Fish, okra & tamarind stew

I dedicate this recipe to my dear friend Bryan Koh. I first met him in Singapore and he took me to some of the best places in town for local cuisine, including fish head curry. Sadly, it isn't something we get to eat very often back home in England, so I came up with a version that we make here to enjoy while thinking of Bryan.

SERVES 4 TO 6

3½oz fresh ginger root, peeled

1oz fresh turmeric, unpeeled
    and scrubbed

1 onion, cut into coarse chunks

4 garlic cloves, peeled

vegetable oil, for frying

3 cardamom pods, bashed

1 teaspoon cumin seeds

1 teaspoon fennel seeds

1 teaspoon chile flakes

1 teaspoon ground coriander

1 teaspoon ground turmeric

10½oz fresh okra (or use frozen
    whole okra, defrosted)

3 tomatoes, coarsely diced

1 tablespoon unsweetened
    tamarind paste

1lb 2oz skinless chunky white fish
    fillet, such as cod, hake, or
    haddock, cut into 1½-inch chunks

sea salt flakes and generous amount
    of freshly ground black pepper

Put the ginger, fresh turmeric, onion, and garlic into a mini food processor and blitz to as fine a paste as you can achieve.

Place a saucepan over medium heat, drizzle in a little vegetable oil, and add the paste. Cook for 8 to 10 minutes until all the moisture has evaporated and the paste has mixed with the oil. Stir occasionally to ensure it doesn't stick.

Add the dry spices and salt and pepper and stir. Add the okra and stir to coat it in the mixture, then stir in the tomatoes and tamarind paste. Pour in just enough water to cover the ingredients, cover the pan with a lid, and let simmer over very low heat for 30 minutes until the sauce thickens, stirring occasionally to prevent sticking. If you still have quite a bit of liquid left in the pan, remove the lid and cook over slightly higher heat for a few minutes until reduced.

Place the fish chunks onto the stew, cover with the lid, and cook for 5 minutes. Remove the lid, spoon the okra and sauce over the fish, and cook for a further 5 minutes uncovered. Serve with rice.

SIMPLY DELICIOUS WITH...

Adas Polow (see page 101).

Seafood, coconut & ginger spiced rice

The Spanish have the right idea with their famous pan-baked rice dish of paella, and while this isn't a paella, it's put together in a similar manner, albeit using very different flavors. I am a big lover of rice and I think it makes a fantastic partner for seafood. This spiced coconut and ginger rice is rich, comforting, and has a depth of flavor that makes it incredibly delicious. The best part? You can take it straight from stove to table. This is one-pot cooking at its finest.

SERVES 4 TO 6

2 tablespoons olive oil

1 onion, very finely chopped

3-inch piece of fresh ginger root, peeled and sliced into thin matchsticks

1 cup Spanish paella rice

1 heaped teaspoon curry powder

1 teaspoon ground turmeric

1 cup coconut milk

1 cup cold water

7oz frozen squid tubes, defrosted and each cut into 3 to 4 rings

7oz baby plum tomatoes, halved

6 large raw shrimp in their shells

sea salt flakes and freshly ground black pepper

Place a wide pan, ideally nonstick, over medium heat and pour in the olive oil. Add the onion and cook for a few minutes until it begins to turn translucent. Add the ginger, stirring to ensure it doesn't burn. Continue cooking gently until both the onion and ginger are softened, without browning.

Add the rice and stir until well coated with the onion and ginger, then stir in the curry powder, turmeric, and a generous amount of salt and pepper.

Pour in the coconut milk, cold water, squid, and tomatoes and mix well. Lay the shrimp on top, reduce the heat slightly, and cook gently for about 20 minutes. Cover the pan with a lid and cook for a further 10 minutes until the shrimp turn pink. Then remove the lid and cook for a final 10 minutes until the rice is cooked through. Serve immediately.

SIMPLY DELICIOUS WITH...

Carrot, Pistachio & Dill Weed Salad with Lime & Honey Dressing (see page 51) or Fennel Salad with Spinach, Cashew & Coriander Seed Dressing (see page 53).

Something special

Crispy cod wraps *with salsa & harissa lime mayo*

I sometimes find that fish can be a bit of a hard sell to some folks, but this is the perfect recipe for converting fussy eaters.

MAKES 6

2 eggs

¾ cup all-purpose flour

1 tablespoon garlic granules

1 tablespoon powdered mustard

2 teaspoons paprika

1 teaspoon cayenne pepper

1 teaspoon ground turmeric

vegetable oil, for frying

1lb 2oz cod loins, cut into
   1-inch chunks

6 mini tortilla wraps

sea salt flakes and black pepper

FOR THE SALSA

2 tomatoes, very finely diced

½ onion, very finely diced

½ small pack (about ½oz) dill weed,
   chopped

drizzle of olive oil

1 teaspoon superfine sugar

FOR THE HARISSA LIME MAYO

3 tablespoons mayonnaise

1 tablespoon rose harissa

finely grated zest of 1 lime and juice of ½

sea salt flakes

First make the salsa. Combine the tomatoes, onion, and dill weed in a bowl. Add the olive oil and sugar and season well with salt and pepper. Mix everything together and set aside.

Mix the mayonnaise ingredients together in a small bowl and set aside.

Crack the eggs into a small shallow bowl, season with a little salt and pepper, and beat together. Put the flour, garlic granules, powder, and spices into a separate small shallow bowl. Season very generously with salt and generously with pepper and mix until well combined.

Pour enough vegetable oil into a deep skillet to fill to a depth of ¾ inch. Heat the oil over medium-high heat and bring to frying temperature. Line a plate with paper towels.

Coat each piece of fish evenly in the flour mixture, then dip into the beaten egg to coat, and finally dip once more in the flour mixture, ensuring each piece is well coated. Test if the oil is ready by dipping a piece of fish into it. If it sizzles immediately, it is hot enough. If it bubbles ferociously, the oil is too hot, so reduce the heat before you begin cooking. Fry the fish in batches for about 2 to 3 minutes, or until the batter is crispy and deep golden brown. Transfer to the lined plate to drain. Serve in wraps with the mayo and top with a little of the salsa.

SIMPLY DELICIOUS WITH... Baked Sweet Potato Fries with Za'atar & Garlic (see page 34).

Sticky peach & halloumi skewers

I love halloumi so much I am always trying to come up with quick and easy ways to make it shine. It's a refrigerator staple in my house. When I'm really exhausted I tend to turn to halloumi, so I have learned to be a bit creative with it. This recipe, like so many of my recipes, was born out of convenience. A simple kitchen-cupboard and spice-rack raid, and suddenly the humble halloumi is transformed into something utterly indulgent. This also happens to make for great sharing or finger food.

MAKES 12

2 x 9oz blocks of halloumi cheese

¼ heaped cup apricot or peach jam

1 teaspoon chile flakes

1 heaped teaspoon dried wild thyme

1 teaspoon garlic granules

olive oil, for frying

2 tablespoons cold water

3 large ripe peaches (or nectarines), stoned and cut into 8 wedges

freshly ground black pepper

Cut each block of halloumi in half lengthwise, then cut each half into 3 equal-sized cubes to make 12 cubes in total.

Put the jam, chile flakes, thyme, garlic granules, and a generous amount of pepper into a small bowl and mix together until evenly combined.

Place a skillet over medium heat and brush the pan with a little olive oil to just lightly coat the bottom. Add the halloumi cubes and fry for about 1 minute on each side until nicely browned all over, then remove from the pan and set aside. Rinse or wipe out the pan with paper towels.

Add the jam mixture to the pan along with the measured cold water. Stir it over the heat until it reaches a glaze consistency. Return the halloumi to the pan and turn to coat with the glaze, then remove the pan from the heat.

Take 12 small skewers and thread each with a wedge of peach (or nectarine), then a cube of halloumi followed by another wedge of peach to finish. Serve immediately.

SIMPLY DELICIOUS WITH...

Crispy Shrimp with Mango & Tomato Dip (see page 164) or Harissa Chicken Noodle Lettuce Cups (see page 115).

Crispy shrimp *with mango & tomato dip*

Salt and pepper squid has always been a favorite of mine, but I'd never thought of giving shrimp the same treatment until I first saw them on a restaurant menu. I've since experimented with different spice coatings on all kinds of fish and seafood, and this is a lovely combination that works really well with the accompanying dip.

SERVES 2

¼ cup cornstarch

1 heaped teaspoon ground turmeric

1 heaped teaspoon garlic granules

1 heaped teaspoon curry powder

1 teaspoon paprika

16 raw jumbo shrimp, shell removed
    but tail left on

vegetable oil, for frying

generous amount of sea salt flakes and
    freshly ground black pepper

FOR THE MANGO & TOMATO DIP

1 ripe tomato

handful of very ripe mango flesh

1¼-inch piece of fresh ginger root, peeled
    and coarsely chopped

2 tablespoons tomato ketchup

1 tablespoon Tabasco sauce

1 tablespoon superfine sugar

sea salt flakes and freshly ground black pepper

Put all the ingredients for the dip into a blender and blitz until smooth. Transfer to a bowl.

Combine the dry ingredients, including the salt and pepper. Add the shrimp and coat well.

Pour enough vegetable oil into a large, deep skillet or saucepan to fill to a depth of about 1 inch. Heat the oil over medium-high heat and bring to frying temperature. (Carefully dip one of the shrimp in the oil. If it sizzles immediately, the oil is ready). Line a plate with a double layer of paper towels.

Fry the shrimp in batches for a few minutes (1 minute for small shrimp, and up to 3 minutes for jumbo, as pictured), or until crisp, golden, and cooked through. Remove the crispy shrimp with a slotted spoon and transfer to the lined plate to drain. Serve immediately with the dip.

SIMPLY DELICIOUS WITH...
Scallion Salad with Sesame & Pul Biber (see page 41) or Corn, Black Bean & Avocado Salad (see page 139).

TIP
If your mango isn't ripe, try adding some mango chutney or apricot jam to bolster the sweetness of the dip.

Spiced pork wraps
with green apple salsa

Pork and apple is a classic combination. The sweet yet tangy apple certainly does so much to complement the meat, but pack in some spices and you take it to a whole other level. Think of these as a kind of taco. Messy, gratifying, and utterly delicious, it's one of my favorite things to eat. Many of the foods I love best are those that can be eaten using your hands and also those where the finished components can be plated up and served to guests so that you can all pile in and it becomes a shared, convivial meal together.

SERVES 4 TO 6

1¾lb boneless pork shoulder,
   cut into 1-inch cubes
vegetable oil
8 to 12 mini tortilla wraps
   (or pitta bread or flatbread)
¼ head of iceberg lettuce,
   very finely shredded
sea salt flakes and
   freshly ground black pepper

FOR THE MARINADE
4 to 5 tablespoons hot chile sauce,
   such as Tabasco or Sriracha, to taste
3 tablespoons superfine sugar
2 tablespoons rice vinegar
1 teaspoon smoked paprika
1 teaspoon ground coriander
1 teaspoon ground cumin
1 teaspoon ground cinnamon

FOR THE SALSA
2 green apples, cored and very
   finely diced
1 small pack (about 1oz) of fresh
   cilantro, very finely chopped
1 small red onion, minced
½ teaspoon nigella seeds
1 tablespoon liquid honey
1 tablespoon olive oil

TO SERVE
Greek yogurt
sweet chilli sauce

CONTINUED OVERLEAF

Put all the ingredients for the marinade into a plastic food container with a generous amount of salt and pepper and mix together well. Add the pork and use your hands to coat it in the marinade. Massage the meat a little to allow the marinade to seep into the pores of the pork. Seal the container with the lid and place in the refrigerator to marinate for a few hours, or overnight.

Preheat the oven to 350°F.

Mix all the salsa ingredients together in a small bowl, season to taste with salt and pepper, and set aside.

Place a skillet over high heat and add a drizzle of vegetable oil. Once hot, use tongs to add a batch of the marinated pieces of pork to the skillet without overcrowding. Leave as much of the marinade behind as you can otherwise it will burn and also cause the meat to stew instead of fry. Cook for 1 to 2 minutes until you have a nice dark crust on the underside, then turn the meat over and cook on the other side for 1 to 2 minutes until cooked through. Remove from the skillet and cook the remaining meat in the same way.

Meanwhile, wrap your tortillas or chosen breads in foil and warm through in the oven.

Place a little shredded lettuce onto each wrap, add the pork and some salsa, then top with a little dollop of Greek yogurt and a drizzle of sweet chilli sauce. Serve immediately.

SIMPLY DELICIOUS WITH...

Scallion Salad with Sesame & Pul Biber (see page 41) and Baked Sweet Potato Fries with Za'atar & Garlic (see page 34).

Chicken & apricot pastries

Growing up in a nation that makes savory pies and pastries like no other means constantly craving and coming up with new and interesting fillings to wrap in a variety of different pastries to keep myself satisfied. The first time I made these was when I had leftover roast chicken and construction workers had set up scaffolding outside my apartment. Let's just say it was the perfect welcoming gesture that kept them friendly and kind for the duration of our relationship.

MAKES 8

vegetable oil

1 large onion, finely chopped

¾lb boneless, skinless chicken thighs

2 teaspoons curry powder

1 teaspoon ground turmeric

1 teaspoon ground cinnamon

½ cup ready-to-eat dried apricots, very thinly sliced

1 tablespoon apricot jam

juice of ½ lemon

1 small pack (about 1oz) of flat leaf parsley, finely chopped

2 x 11oz ready-rolled all-butter puff pastry sheets

1 egg, beaten

1 teaspoon nigella seeds

sea salt flakes and freshly ground black pepper

Place a large saucepan over medium heat and pour in enough vegetable oil to coat the bottom of the pan. Add the onion and cook for a few minutes until softened and translucent, without browning.

Add the chicken, spices, and salt and pepper and stir to coat the chicken well. Pour in enough boiling water to cover the ingredients, then simmer over very low heat for 1 hour until the chicken is cooked through and tender. Remove from the heat and let cool.

Remove the chicken from the pan and finely chop, then put into a bowl. Add the apricots, jam, and lemon juice, along with the remaining sauce from the pan and the parsley, then using your hands, mix well to ensure the chicken is thoroughly coated.

CONTINUED OVERLEAF

Preheat the oven to 425°F. Line a large baking pan with nonstick parchment paper.

Cut each pastry sheet into 4 squares. Divide the chicken mixture into 8 and form into sausage shapes. Lay a sausage shape diagonally on each pastry square, then fold over or gather up the corners of each pastry square and pinch together to seal. Place seam-side down on the prepared baking pan, brush with the beaten egg, and sprinkle with the nigella seeds. Bake for 20 to 22 minutes until a deep golden color. Let cool slightly before serving.

SIMPLY DELICIOUS WITH...

Green-yogurt-dressed Baby Romaine Lettuce with Burnt Hazelnuts (see page 44) and Carrot, Pistachio & Dill Weed Salad with Lime & Honey Dressing (see page 51).

Pear, chickpea & green leaf salad
with maple harissa dressing

I love using fresh fruit in salads, from apples and oranges to luscious ripe berries, but the intense sweetness of pears means they can stand up to much bolder flavors like blue cheese and, most valuable to me, chile and spice. This is a great combination and the addition of chickpeas makes it ever so much more than a salad. The maple syrup and harissa works like magic as a dressing, and I promise you, this is a wonderful addition to any table.

SERVES 4 TO 6

1½ cups arugula, tightly packed

1¾ cups watercress

2 pears, halved, cored, and
   thinly sliced

14oz can chickpeas, drained
   and rinsed

handful of sunflower seeds, to garnish

FOR THE DRESSING

1 generous tablespoon maple syrup

1 tablespoon olive oil

juice of ½ lemon

1 teaspoon rose harissa

generous amount of sea salt flakes and
   freshly ground black pepper

Arrange the salad leaves, pear slices, and chickpeas in a large shallow bowl or on a platter.

Mix all the dressing ingredients together in a measuring cup or small bowl and then pour it over the salad. Sprinkle with the sunflower seeds to garnish and serve immediately.

SIMPLY DELICIOUS WITH...

Chorizo, Goat Cheese & Cumin Borek (see page 148) or Goat Cheese, Vegetable & Za'atar Filo Tart (see page 207).

Cauliflower & asparagus black rice salad

Cauliflower makes an absolutely superb addition to a salad, and here I've paired it with my other love, rice, in particular, beautiful dark black rice. Any leftovers make the most wonderful packed lunch the next day, if there are any leftovers, of course.

SERVES 6 TO 8

1 cup black Venus rice

1¾ cups water

1 cauliflower, cut into florets

9oz asparagus tips

1¼ cups coarsely chopped fresh
   cilantro

½ cup coarsely chopped dill weed,
   plus extra to garnish

½ cup coarsely chopped
   flat leaf parsley

6 tablespoons olive oil, divided

1 cup plain yogurt

squeeze of lemon juice

2 to 3 preserved lemons, to taste

½ teaspoon pul biber chile flakes

sea salt flakes and freshly ground
   black pepper

Put the rice and the water in a saucepan and bring to a boil, then cover, reduce the heat, and let simmer for 35 to 45 minutes, or following the package directions, until tender.

Meanwhile, cook the cauliflower florets in a separate pan of boiling water for 10 minutes, then drain and rinse under cold running water. Set aside. Blanch the asparagus tips in another pan of boiling water for 3 minutes, then plunge into cold water to cool. Let drain.

Put the cilantro, dill weed, and parsley into a mini food processor with 4 tablespoons of the olive oil and ⅓ cup cold water and blitz until smooth. Season well with salt and pepper, then stir into the yogurt in a bowl and add the lemon juice. Set aside.

Place a nonstick ridged grill pan over high heat. Drizzle the asparagus with the remaining olive oil and rub it in. Chargrill the asparagus for 2 minutes on each side, then set aside.

Arrange the rice on a platter, top with the cauliflower and asparagus, and dollop with the yogurt mixture. Thinly slice the preserved lemons and arrange on top, then sprinkle with the pul biber and garnish with dill weed before serving.

SIMPLY DELICIOUS WITH...

Turmeric Chicken Kebabs (see page 24) and Yogurt & Spice Roasted Salmon (see page 62).

Roasted parsnips
with tahini yogurt sauce, herb oil & pomegranate seeds

I've always thought of parsnips as one of my favorite root vegetables, and I can't understand why the British only eat them at Christmas. My friend Mathew hates parsnips, and while I did win him over with the harissa and honey-roasted parsnips in my book, *Bazaar*, I am hoping this will seal the deal and put parsnips firmly on the menu for him.

SERVES 4 TO 6

2¼lb parsnips, peeled and halved
    lengthwise
garlic oil, for drizzling
2 sprigs of tarragon, leaves picked
4 sprigs of flat leaf parsley
3 to 4 tablespoons olive oil
2 squeezes of lemon juice

1 tablespoon tahini
1 to 2 tablespoons warm water
¼ cup Greek yogurt
⅓ cup pomegranate seeds
sea salt flakes and freshly ground
    black pepper

Preheat the oven to 400°F.

Place the parsnips on a large baking pan, drizzle with garlic oil, and season with a generous amount of salt and pepper. Mix the parsnips around with your hands until they are well coated in the oil and seasoning, then spread them out on the pan. Roast in the oven for about 30 to 35 minutes (depending on their size and thickness) until nicely browned and tender.

Meanwhile, put the tarragon and parsley into a blender with the olive oil, a squeeze of the lemon juice, and the salt and pepper and blitz until you have a smooth herb oil. Set aside.

To make the sauce, in a small bowl, mix together the tahini, the remaining squeeze of lemon juice, and 1 tablespoon of warm water (not cold water, otherwise the tahini will seize). Then beat in the yogurt and season to taste with salt. Add another tablespoon of warm water if you prefer a thinner consistency.

Once the parsnips are done, arrange them on a platter and drizzle first with the tahini yogurt sauce, then with the herb oil. Finally, sprinkle with the pomegranate seeds before serving.

SIMPLY DELICIOUS WITH...
Spice-rubbed Spatchcocked Squab (see page 55) or Pot-roasted Brisket with Harissa & Spices (see page 59).

Strawberry, soft goat cheese & pistachio salad

In the early 1990s I once made a salad using strawberries to impress my friends. I must admit it went down like a lead balloon, being perhaps too avant garde at the time. This recipe, however, is one I created with confidence and have served several times. When the strawberries are in season and bursting with sweetness they dress the salad with their natural juices. The soft, mild goat cheese works so well with the strawberries, and pistachios add not only a vibrant color, but also a wonderful crunch. It's a perfect summer salad to go with any meal.

SERVES 4 TO 6

14oz strawberries

5 basil leaves

5 large mint leaves

5½oz soft, mild rindless goat cheese, torn into small chunks

½ cup coarsely chopped pistachio nuts

½ teaspoon sumac

½ teaspoon pul biber chile flakes

freshly ground black pepper

FOR THE DRESSING

2 tablespoons olive oil

juice of ½ lemon

1 generous tablespoon liquid honey

Hull the strawberries and then cut them into quarters. Stack the basil leaves, roll them up together, and then finely slice the roll widthwise to cut the basil into thin ribbons. Repeat with the mint leaves.

Arrange the strawberries on a platter and scatter them with the goat cheese and herbs. Add the pistachios and sprinkle with the sumac and pul biber.

Mix the dressing ingredients together in a measuring cup or small bowl. Season the salad with plenty of pepper, then drizzle with the dressing to serve.

SIMPLY DELICIOUS WITH...

Green Chicken (see page 23) or Harissa Kofta Lettuce Cups with Preserved Lemon Yogurt (see page 123).

TIP

Try substituting feta for the goat cheese.

Spiced Belgian endive & roasted bell pepper salad *with oranges & anchovies*

This is also known as Rob's Birthday Salad since I created this for the special birthday of a good friend of mine. I've never met anyone who was so into anchovies (I myself am a relatively new convert). This salad embodies all the flavors and components—bitter, sweet, sharp, and nutty—that I feel complement the saltiness of the anchovies.

SERVES 4 TO 6

10½oz baby bell peppers, halved, cored, and seeded

4 oranges

2 large heads of Belgian endive, leaves separated

2oz anchovy fillets

generous handful of pine nuts

sea salt flakes and black pepper

FOR THE DRESSING

3 tablespoons olive oil, plus extra for drizzling

2 tablespoons red wine vinegar

1 generous tablespoon liquid honey

1 heaped teaspoon ground coriander

1 heaped teaspoon paprika

Preheat your oven to its highest setting. Line a large baking pan with nonstick parchment paper.

Place the bell pepper halves skin-side up on the prepared baking pan and roast for about 12 to 14 minutes, or until nicely charred. Remove from the oven, turn the peppers over, and let cool.

Using a sharp knife, cut a disk of peel off of the top and bottom of each orange in turn. Then, working from the top of the fruit downward, cut away the remaining peel and pith in strips until the entire orange is peeled. Slice each orange widthwise into 4 or 5 slices and then cut the slices in half into semicircles.

Mix the dressing ingredients together in a small bowl and season well with salt and pepper.

Once the bell peppers have cooled, place them in a bowl, add the dressing, and toss to coat.

Arrange the Belgian endive leaves, orange slices, and bell peppers on a large platter and top with the anchovies. Sprinkle with the pine nuts and season with salt and pepper before serving.

SIMPLY DELICIOUS WITH...

Fragrant Fish Cakes with Preserved Lemon Mayonnaise (see page 152) and Crispy Cod Wraps with Salsa & Harissa Lime Mayo (see page 160).

Smoked eggplant, tomato, tamarind & peanut salad

Smoking eggplant is a classic Middle Eastern technique, but this recipe is quite different to any other. I must confess that the first time I made it, I ate the whole thing! Any recipe that has texture and a combination of savory, sweet, and sour is always a winner in my view. I like simple dishes that burst with flavor, and this one does just that.

SERVES 6 TO 8

4 eggplant

3 large tomatoes, each cut into 6, or 10 cherry tomatoes, halved

2 tablespoons superfine sugar

1 heaped tablespoon unsweetened tamarind paste

1 tablespoon vegan red wine vinegar

2 shallots, halved and thinly sliced into half moons

2 tablespoons olive oil

2 generous handfuls of salted peanuts, coarsely chopped

sea salt flakes and freshly ground black pepper

Using long-handled tongs, blister and char the eggplant either on a barbecue or over the flame of a gas stove. Blacken the skins all over and cook them until they have collapsed in size by half.

Place the eggplant on a heatproof surface or platter and let stand for about 20 minutes until cool enought to handle. Keeping the stalks intact, split them lengthwise in half. Use a large metal spoon to scoop out all the flesh into a fine-mesh sieve to drain off the excess juices, discarding the charred skins.

Once drained, tip the eggplant flesh into a mixing bowl, add the remaining ingredients, except the olive oil and peanuts, and use a fork to mix together thoroughly. Season generously with salt and pepper, then add the olive oil and mix well. Finally, stir in the peanuts and serve. This salad is great served as part of a feast or with barbecued meats.

SIMPLY DELICIOUS WITH...

Tepsi Kebap (see page 84) or Lamb, Cumin, Cilantro & Chile Kebabs (see page 118).

TIP

If using a gas stove to char the eggplant, first line your stove with foil to avoid a messy clean-up job.

Spiced pork stew

When slow-cooked, pork shoulder falls apart but the fat it contains means it remains juicy. Pork can really stand up to spices, and while it may not be a looker, this boldly spiced stew is a comfort staple of mine. The longer you cook it, the more the meat falls apart. And it's so versatile! You can eat it with rice or bread, or pile it into a baked potato. Add beans to any leftovers or use it as a filling for a wrap or even a pie. And it freezes well, too.

SERVES 4 TO 6

vegetable oil

2 onions, finely chopped

2¼lb boneless pork shoulder,
    cut into 1½-inch chunks

3 tablespoons medium curry powder

1 tablespoon garlic granules

1 tablespoon paprika

1 tablespoon ground coriander

1 tablespoon celery salt

2 heaped teaspoons ground allspice

4 to 5 sprigs of thyme, leaves picked

6 fat garlic cloves, thinly sliced

1 Scotch bonnet chile, pierced
    but left whole

4 tomatoes, coarsely diced

4 scallions, thinly sliced

sea salt flakes, if needed, and freshly
    ground black pepper

naan bread, or rice and peas, to serve

Place a large saucepan over medium-high heat and pour in enough vegetable oil to coat the bottom of the pan. Add the onions and cook for a few minutes until softened and translucent, without browning.

Add the pork, curry powder, garlic granules, paprika, coriander, celery salt, allspice, thyme, and a generous amount of pepper. Stir until the meat is well coated in the seasonings, then add the garlic slices, Scotch bonnet chile, tomatoes, and scallions and mix well. Add enough cold water to cover the ingredients, stir, and reduce the heat to medium-low. Cook the stew, uncovered, for 15 minutes, then stir, cover the pan with a lid, and continue to cook for a minimum of 4 hours ensuring you stir it every now and again. (I cook it for 6 hours on very low heat for the best results.) An hour before the end of the cooking time, check and adjust the seasoning and, if necessary, add just enough water to create a saucelike consistency. If after 3 hours' cooking there is a lot of liquid in the pan, remove the lid for the last hour of cooking to reduce. Remove the chile, then serve with naan bread or plain boiled rice and peas.

Spice-seared lamb

with zucchini ribbons, pickled chiles & pine nuts

This perfect summer salad has sharp bursts of flavor from the preserved lemons and pickled chiles in the dressing, and can easily be scaled up to feed a crowd. You can even cook the lamb on the barbecue and make the salad ahead. Just assemble it all before serving.

SERVES 6 TO 8

⅓ cup pine nuts

1 teaspoon fennel seeds

1 teaspoon cumin seeds

1 teaspoon coriander seeds

olive oil

1lb 2oz lamb steaks, ½ inch in
    thickness (about 3 to 4 steaks)

2 small zucchini

4 pickled peppers, thinly sliced

4 preserved lemons, seeded and
    finely chopped

4 to 5 sprigs of parsley, leaves picked

sea salt flakes and freshly ground
    black pepper

Preheat the oven to 400°F. Place the pine nuts in an ovenproof dish and toast in the oven for 6 minutes until golden, then set aside.

Place a skillet over medium-high heat. Add the fennel, cumin, and coriander seeds and toast them, shaking the pan, for 2 minutes until they release their aroma. Transfer the toasted seeds to a mortar and pestle and finely grind, then let cool. Place the pan back on the heat.

Drizzle 2 tablespoons olive oil over the lamb, add the ground spices, and work them into the meat until the steaks are evenly coated with the spice mix. Season both sides with pepper and then sear each steak in the hot skillet for 1 minute on each side, sprinkling each side with just a little salt, until nicely browned. Remove from the pan and let rest.

Using a vegetable peeler, cut the zucchini lengthwise into long, thin ribbons into a mixing bowl. Drizzle with 2 to 3 tablespoons olive oil, then add a generous amount of black pepper, the pickled peppers, preserved lemon, parsley, and toasted pine nuts. Mix together well and then arrange on serving plates. Slice the lamb steaks, lay them on top of each portion, and serve immediately.

SIMPLY DELICIOUS WITH...

Watermelon, Black Olive & Feta with Cayenne, Honey & Lime Dressing (see page 143).

TIP
Toasting the pine nuts in the oven, rather than in a skillet, ensures even toasting.

Marinated steak
with labneh, pul biber butter & crispy onions

Taking inspiration from the Iskender kebap of Turkey, this dish of marinated steak with labneh (or strained yogurt, if you prefer) and pul biber butter is a simple yet effective explosion of flavors. Scoop pillowy flatbread through the yogurt for maximum enjoyment.

SERVES 4 TO 6

1lb to 1lb 2oz sirloin steak, ¾ inch thick, trimmed of excess fat, cut into 1-inch cubes

1 heaped tablespoon dried mint

1 teaspoon garlic granules

1 teaspoon ground cumin

½ teaspoon celery salt

2 tablespoons olive oil

¾ stick butter

2 teaspoons pul biber chile flakes

14oz labneh, or 1¾ cups Greek yogurt strained in a cheesecloth bag overnight (see method on page 11)

generous handful of ready-made crispy fried onions

2 to 3 sprigs of dill weed, very finely chopped

sea salt flakes and freshly ground black pepper

Ensure the steak is at room temperature before cooking.

Put the steak cubes into a mixing bowl along with the dried mint, garlic granules, cumin, celery salt, and a generous amount of pepper. Mix together well. Pour in the olive oil and mix again. Let the meat marinate for about 10 minutes while you heat a large skillet over medium-high heat.

Add the meat cubes to the hot pan and cook for 1 minute on each side, then transfer to a small plate and season with salt. Turn off the heat and wipe the skillet with paper towels. Return the pan to low heat and add the butter. Once melted, add the pul biber. Stir a little until the butter turns red from the chiles, then remove the pan from the heat.

Spread out the labneh or strained Greek yogurt on a large plate. Lift the steak off the plate using a slotted spoon and shake off the excess juices, then arrange on the labneh or yogurt before pouring the spiced butter over the steak. Scatter with the crispy onions followed by the dill weed and serve immediately.

SIMPLY DELICIOUS WITH...
Ultimate Falafels (see page 81) or Polow-e-Bademjan-o-Felfel (see page 125).

Spiced beef pancakes
with chopped egg, dill weed & sour cream

Whenever I think of pancakes or Pancake Day (Shrove Tuesday), I rarely think of maple syrup, unlike many people, and I must admit that I will always choose savory over sweet dishes. These pancakes combine some of my favorite ingredients in every mouthful. And what is really lovely about them is how convivial they are, and so ideal for feasting and sharing. Everyone makes their own combinations and can enjoy them without you having to plate up the pancakes individually.

MAKES 6

4 eggs

vegetable oil, for frying

1lb 2oz ground beef

1 tablespoon garlic granules

1 tablespoon ground cumin

1 tablespoon paprika

½ teaspoon cayenne pepper

½ teaspoon ground cinnamon

2 shallots, minced

1 small pack (about 1oz) of fresh dill
    weed, finely chopped

¾ cup sour cream

sea salt flakes and freshly ground
    black pepper

FOR THE PANCAKES

½ cup all-purpose flour

pinch of salt

1 egg

½ cup milk

1 tablespoon water

2 tablespoons butter, melted

Pour boiling water from a kettle into a saucepan set over medium-high heat. Once the water is bubbling, carefully lower in the eggs and boil for 10 minutes. Drain the eggs and place them under cold running water to stop the cooking process, then let stand in cold water until needed.

Place a large skillet over medium-high heat, drizzle in a little vegetable oil, and add the ground beef. Immediately begin breaking the meat up as finely as you can to avoid clumps. Once the meat has cooked a little, stir in the garlic granules, spices, and a generous amount of pepper. Continue cooking the meat until it is well browned, then season generously with salt. Mix well and remove the pan from the heat.

CONTINUED OVERLEAF

To make the pancakes, preheat the oven to 350°F. Line an ovenproof dish with nonstick parchment paper.

Put the flour, salt, and egg into a large mixing bowl. Stir the milk and water to combine in a measuring cup, then blend into the flour mixture a little at a time, whisking well to beat out any lumps. Mix in the melted butter, then transfer to a large bowl. Place a 7-inch skillet over medium-high heat and drizzle in a tiny amount of vegetable oil. Once the oil is hot, ladle in just enough of the batter to make a thin pancake. Cook for about 1 minute on each side, or until nicely browned. Transfer to the prepared dish, cover with foil, and place in the oven to keep warm while you make the rest of the pancakes.

Peel the hard-boiled eggs and finely chop them, then place in a little bowl. Place the minced shallots, chopped dill weed, and sour cream into three separate bowls.

Briefly reheat the beef mixture over high heat. Once hot, divide it among the pancakes. Top with the egg, shallots, dill weed, and a good dollop of sour cream to serve.

Green bean & black-eyed pea baklava
with feta & honey

I absolutely love a savory baklava. Technically, it's just a vegetable-filled pastry sweetened with a drizzle of syrup, although in this instance laziness prevailed and I switched from my usual syrup to a little liquid honey, which means it's even easier to make. This is one of those perfect all-in-one meals that doesn't need any accompaniment. However, if you really insist, then a crisp green salad on the side would be the ideal partner.

SERVES 8

olive oil

2 onions, halved and thinly sliced
    into half moons

6 fat garlic cloves, thinly sliced

14oz trimmed fine green beans,
    halved in length

3 tablespoons tomato paste

1 teaspoon ground turmeric

1 teaspoon ground cinnamon

1 teaspoon paprika

14oz can chopped tomatoes

2 tablespoons superfine sugar

½ cup cold water

14oz can black-eyed peas, drained and
    ½ the brine reserved

2 tablespoons butter, plus
    3½ tablespoons butter, melted,
    for brushing

6 sheets of filo pastry (each about
    19 x 10 inches)

7oz vegetarian feta cheese, crumbled

sea salt flakes and freshly ground
    black pepper

liquid honey, to serve

Place a large saucepan over medium heat and pour in enough olive oil to coat the bottom of the pan. Add the onions and cook for a few minutes until softened and translucent, without browning. Add the garlic and cook, stirring, for 2 minutes, then add the green beans. Turn the heat up slightly and cook until they soften, stirring regularly.

Add the tomato paste, turmeric, cinnamon, and paprika and stir until the vegetable mixture is well coated. Add the canned tomatoes, the brine from the beans, and the sugar and stir well. Pour in the water and stir again, then reduce the heat to medium-low and let simmer for 20 minutes. Remove the pan from the heat and add the black-eyed peas. Stir through the 2 tablespoons butter, season with salt and pepper, and then set aside to cool completely.

CONTINUED OVERLEAF

Meanwhile, preheat the oven to 400°F.

Select a rectangular ovenproof dish, about 13 x 9 inches, and brush the bottom liberally with some of the melted butter. Line the bottom of the dish with 4 sheets of filo pastry (2 lengthwise and 2 widthwise). Allow an equal amount of pastry to overhang each side of the dish. Brush the pastry with melted butter. Pour in the green bean and black-eyed pea mixture and shake the dish to create an even layer. Then scatter the mixture with the crumbled feta.

Fold the overhanging pastry over the filling. Take the remaining pastry sheets, and fold them so they are slightly larger than the dish. Then place them on top of the dish, tucking the pastry edges down the sides using a round-bladed knife or similar, so the top looks neat and smooth. Brush the top liberally with the remaining melted butter. Using a very sharp knife, cut the top layer of pastry into 8 equal portions (this makes it easier to serve it once cooked). Place the dish in the oven and bake for 30 to 35 minutes until deep golden brown.

Remove from the oven, and cut the baklava along the scored lines into portions. Drizzle each portion with a little honey, as liked, to serve.

SIMPLY DELICIOUS WITH…

Green-yogurt-dressed Baby Romaine Lettuce with Burnt Hazelnuts (see page 44).

Chargrilled saffron squid with chile & charred lemons

Chargrilled squid always reminds me of summer vacations in the Mediterranean. Every time I cook this, I wonder why I don't make it more often, as there is nothing fiddly involved. The crispy garlic, charred chile, and the juice from the charred lemons in this recipe turn this dish into something truly spectacular and flavor-packed.

SERVES 4

vegetable oil, for frying

4 garlic cloves, thinly sliced

8 frozen squid tubes (about 14oz total weight), defrosted

2 pinches of saffron threads

2 lemons, halved

2 long red chiles

1½ cups arugula, tightly packed

olive oil, for drizzling

sea salt flakes and black pepper

Line a plate with a double layer of paper towels. Pour enough vegetable oil into a small saucepan to fill to a depth of about ½ inch. Add the garlic slices and fry over medium-low heat for a few minutes until lightly golden (avoid browning otherwise they will taste bitter). Remove with a slotted spoon and transfer to the lined plate to drain.

Using a sharp knife, cut down one side of each squid tube and open it out flat on the cutting board with the outside facing up. Score the outside flesh gently in diagonal lines about ½ inch apart, first in one direction and then in the opposite direction, to create a diamond pattern. Cut in half so that you get 2 pieces from each squid body. Place all the squid pieces in a small bowl or food bag. Crumble in the saffron, and rub it into the squid. Cover the bowl with plastic wrap or seal the bag and place in the refrigerator to marinate for 1 hour.

Heat a nonstick ridged grill pan over high heat. Once hot, chargrill the squid for 2 to 3 minutes on each side, then remove from the pan and transfer to a plate. Add the chiles and the lemons (cut-side down to the grill pan and cook, turning the chiles frequently until charred all over.

Arrange the arugula on plates with the chargrilled squid pieces, then thinly slice the charred chiles and scatter them over the squid. Drizzle with olive oil, season with salt and pepper, scatter with the fried garlic slices, and serve with the charred lemon halves.

SIMPLY DELICIOUS WITH...

Cauliflower & Asparagus Black Rice Salad (see page 174) or Harissa Kofta Lettuce Cups (see page 123).

Firecracker shrimp

I absolutely love shrimp and they would most definitely always be part of my ideal meal. And the larger they are, the more I love them. The first time I did this, I managed to find the most enormous shrimp, which made the finished dish utterly spectacular. But I recommend only using what is easy for you to get hold of. And yes, if you don't like the shells, you can use peeled shrimp, although go for the very best quality you can find. The sauce —punchy, fiery, fruity, and aromatic—is everything I love. A little rice on the side or even some bread to mop up the juices would complete the picture.

SERVES 4 TO 6

2 oranges

2 to 3 tablespoons olive oil

4 fat garlic cloves, thinly sliced

4-inch piece of fresh ginger root, peeled and finely grated

8 raw jumbo shrimp in their shell, about 2½oz each (or use 12 smaller ones)

3 tablespoons Sriracha

generous handful of marjoram leaves (or use 1 tablespoon dried marjoram if that's all you can find), plus extra to garnish

2 tablespoons butter

sea salt flakes and freshly ground black pepper

Using a vegetable peeler, peel the rind of the oranges, then slice into thin strips. Squeeze and reserve the juice.

Heat your largest skillet or wok over high heat. Once hot, add the olive oil, quickly followed by the garlic and ginger. Stir-fry for a few seconds without letting them burn. Add the shrimp and toss them in the garlic and ginger. When they begin to cook (the cooking time will vary depending on the size of shrimp you use, but watch for them to turn pinkish white), stir in the orange rind strips, then add the Sriracha and orange juice. Stir until the shrimp are well coated in the mixture, then season well with salt and pepper and add the marjoram.

Cook the sauce for several minutes, stirring if necessary to stop the shrimp from sticking, until it is reduced and turns sticky and the shrimp are cooked through. Stir in the butter, and once melted, turn the shrimp over one last time to coat them in the sauce. Serve immediately, garnished with extra marjoram leaves if liked.

SIMPLY DELICIOUS WITH...

Tomato & Garlic Rice (see page 38) or Adas Polow (see page 101).

Chard, ricotta & runny egg pie

This pie brings several of my loves together: bitter greens, cheese, and a good runny egg. If you can't find chard, use spinach, arugula, or your favorite leafy greens.

SERVES 6 TO 8

olive oil

14oz chard, stalks thinly sliced and
    leaves coarsely chopped

7oz cabbage leaves or collard
    greens, stalks removed and
    leaves coarsely shredded

2 tablespoons garlic granules

1 tablespoon ground coriander

1 heaped tablespoon sumac

2 cups ricotta cheese

¾ stick butter, melted

7 sheets of filo pastry (each
    about 19 x 10 inches)

6 eggs

1 teaspoon nigella seeds

sea salt flakes and freshly ground
    black pepper

Place a large saucepan over medium heat, and pour in enough olive oil to coat the bottom of the pan. Add the chard stalks and cook for a few minutes until softened, then add the chard leaves and the cabbage. Stir-fry for a few minutes until beginning to soften. Add the garlic granules and coriander and cook for several minutes, stirring occasionally, until the leaves are wilted and cooked through. Season very generously (it will need overseasoning at this stage) and stir well. Add the sumac and stir well to combine. Remove from the heat and let cool.

Preheat the oven to 400°F.

Fold the ricotta into the cooled greens mixture and check and adjust the seasoning.

Select an ovenproof dish, about 13 x 9 inches, and brush the bottom liberally with melted butter. Line the bottom of the dish with 4 sheets of filo pastry (2 lengthwise and 2 widthwise) allowing an equal amount of pastry to overhang each side of the dish. Brush the top layer with melted butter. Pour the ricotta mixture into the buttered filo pastry and spread it out into an even layer. Make 6 holes in the mixture and crack an egg into each. Season the eggs with a little pepper, then gently lay a pastry sheet over to cover the entire filling. Fold the overhanging pastry over the filling and lightly brush the edges with more melted butter. Cut the remaining 2 pastry sheets in half, crumple up each piece, and arrange them on top of the pie. Brush generously with the remaining melted butter and sprinkle with nigella seeds.

Bake the pie for 20 to 25 minutes until golden brown. For well cooked eggs, reduce the oven temperature to 350°F, and cook for a further 30 minutes before serving.

Grilled pineapple & potato kari

One of the joys of spices is that they perfectly complement anything containing a little sweetness, giving your palate a pleasing balance. A little acidity never goes amiss when pairing spice with sweet, and this curry hits all those notes beautifully. It may feel a little adventurous for some to combine fruit with stews and curries, but it's nothing new. Many cultures have been doing it for centuries, and for good reason. It's absolutely delicious!

SERVES 6

2 tablespoons vegetable oil, plus
    extra for brushing
1 teaspoon cumin seeds
1 teaspoon fennel seeds
1 teaspoon black mustard seeds
1 large onion, coarsely chopped
1 teaspoon ground cinnamon
1 teaspoon ground turmeric

1 to 2 small green chiles, split
    lengthwise but kept whole
14oz can chopped tomatoes
1lb 2oz baby new potatoes
1 large pineapple
sea salt flakes and freshly ground
    black pepper
rice or flatbread, to serve

Place a large saucepan over medium heat, pour in 2 tablespoons vegetable oil, and add all the seeds. Once they sizzle, add the onion and cook for a few minutes until softened, then stir in the cinnamon, turmeric, a generous amount of salt and pepper, and the chiles. Cook for 1 minute.

Add the canned tomatoes, then fill the can with cold water, pour into the pan, and stir. Bring to a boil and add the potatoes whole (if they are large, cut them into 1¼-inch chunks before adding). Stir well, reduce the heat, and simmer for 30 to 35 minutes until the potatoes are cooked through, adding a little more water or covering the pan with a lid to maintain the liquid level.

Meanwhile, peel and core the pineapple, then cut the flesh into 1½-inch chunks. Heat a nonstick ridged grill pan over high heat. Brush each pineapple chunk with a little oil, add to the hot pan, and cook for 1 minute on each side until charred.

Once the potatoes in the curry are cooked, fish out and discard the chiles. Stir in the charred pineapple pieces, heat the mixture through, and then serve with rice or flatbread.

SIMPLY DELICIOUS WITH...

Flame-roasted Bell Pepper, Pistachio & Dill Weed Yogurt (see page 42) or Chargrilled Eggplant (see page 140).

Red kidney bean & sweet potato stew *with yogurt & hot mint oil*

The yogurt in this vegetarian stew offers a perfect, cooling contrast, and the hot mint oil—a very Persian addition we call nana daagh—finishes the dish incredibly well. You can serve this with rice or bread, and leftovers make an excellent brunch dish with poached eggs.

SERVES 4 TO 6

vegetable oil, for frying

1 large onion, diced

4 fat garlic cloves, thinly sliced

2 teaspoons cumin seeds

1 teaspoon ground cinnamon

1 teaspoon ground turmeric

1 teaspoon chile flakes

3 cups tomato puree

1lb 2oz sweet potatoes, peeled and
   cut into ½-inch chunks

14oz can red kidney beans, drained

1 small pack (about 1oz) of flat leaf
   parsley, coarsely chopped

1 tablespoon dried mint

¾ cup Greek yogurt

sea salt flakes and freshly ground
   black pepper

Place a large saucepan over medium heat and pour in enough oil to coat the bottom of the pan. Add the onion and cook for a few minutes until it begins to turn translucent, then add the garlic, stirring to ensure it doesn't burn. Continue cooking until both have softened, without browning. Add the spices and stir to coat the onion mixture in them. Let it cook, stirring continuously, for a minute or so. Season generously with salt and pepper to taste, then stir in the passata. Reduce the heat to low and let simmer gently, uncovered, for about 25 to 30 minutes.

Stir the sweet potato chunks into the stew and cook for a further 20 minutes or so until the sweet potato is tender. Then add the beans and most of the parsley and heat through.

Place a separate pan over medium heat, add the dried mint and 1 tablespoon vegetable oil. Heat the mint for a few minutes, without letting it burn. Remove the pan from the heat.

Transfer the stew to bowls, add dollops of the yogurt around the dish, and scatter with the remaining parsley. Pour the hot mint oil evenly over the stew and serve immediately.

SIMPLY DELICIOUS WITH...

Adas Polow (see page 101).

Goat cheese, vegetable & za'atar filo tart

Think of this as a sort of quiche but with a filo pastry crust instead—the perfect match for the rich, creamy goat cheese filling, spiked with the heady fragrance of za'atar.

SERVES 6 TO 8

vegetable oil

1 eggplant, finely diced

1 red bell pepper, cored, seeded, and finely diced

1 zucchini, finely diced

3½ tablespoons butter, melted

6 sheets of filo pastry (each about 19 x 10 inches)

7 eggs, 1 beaten, to glaze

1¼ cups heavy cream

2 tablespoons za'atar

1 teaspoon garlic granules

9oz rindless soft goat cheese, torn into coarse chunks

sea salt flakes and black pepper

Preheat the oven to 400°F.

Line a platter with a double layer of paper towels. Place a large saucepan over high heat and pour in enough vegetable oil to coat the bottom of the pan. Add the diced eggplant, mix with the oil, and cook for several minutes until it begins to brown, stirring occasionally. Add the red bell pepper and cook for a few minutes until softened. Finally, add the zucchini and cook for 6 to 8 minutes, stirring occasionally. Remove the vegetables with a slotted spoon. Shake any excess oil off of them, then transfer to the lined platter to drain and cool.

Meanwhile, select an ovenproof dish, about 13 x 9 inches. Brush melted butter over each pastry sheet and place 2 layers lengthwise in the dish with the ends overhanging the short edges of the dish. Take the remaining 4 sheets and set 2 layers side by side widthwise across the dish so that they meet in the center, with the excess overhanging the long edges of the dish. Crumple the overhanging pastry inside the edges of the dish to create a border for your pie, leaving room for the filling. Brush the crumpled pastry with the beaten egg.

Beat the remaining 6 eggs and fold in the cream, za'atar, and garlic granules, followed by the cooked vegetables. Season with salt and pepper. Pour the mixture into the filo base, scatter with the goat cheese, and bake for 30 minutes until golden brown.

SIMPLY DELICIOUS WITH...

Pear, Chickpea & Green Leaf Salad with Maple Harissa Dressing (see page 172).

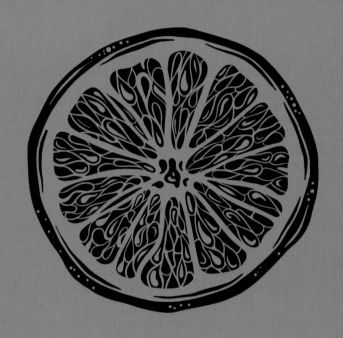

Cakes, bakes & sweet treats

Stuffed dates
with torched goat cheese, pistachios & honey

Dates are very important in Middle Eastern cuisine, but I've only ever really enjoyed them when married with something savory. Here, the slightly acidic yet creamy, mild soft goat cheese is the perfect pairing, along with a little drizzle of honey and the satisfying crunch of the king of Persian nuts, the wonderful pistachio.

MAKES 12

12 large dates
9oz rindless soft goat cheese
1 generous tablespoon liquid honey
3 tablespoons pistachio slivers (or
    whole nuts, finely blitzed in a food
    processor or very finely chopped)

Using a sharp knife, carefully cut along one side of each date in turn, ensuring not to split them in half. Open each date out and remove the stone.

Cut the goat cheese into 12 equal pieces. Roll each one into a ball and then elongate into a sausage shape that will fit snugly into the cavity of a date. Fill all the dates with the goat cheese, set on a plate, and then put into the freezer to firm up.

After 20 minutes, remove the dates from the freezer. Using a chef's kitchen torch, run the flame over the cheese-filled area of each stuffed date for a few seconds until slightly charred. Once all the dates are done, arrange them on a platter, drizzle with a very thin stream of the honey, scatter with the pistachios, and serve with black tea infused with mint leaves, Middle-Eastern style.

Barberry fool

If you're in need of a foolproof, super-quick dessert, then this is the one. While Persians never use barberries in desserts, I am an experimenter and one who likes to get the best from the ingredients I buy. Barberries have a wonderfully sour nature that makes them incredibly versatile in cooking, marinades, butter compounds, and even drinks. So why not in a dessert? This is one of those ridiculously easy recipes that's a perfect quick fix for when you want a sweet treat but prefer to put all the effort into making the savories instead.

SERVES 6

2oz dried barberries, plus extra
    to decorate
¼ cup boiling water
2½ cups heavy cream
⅓ cup confectioner's sugar
¼ cup Greek yogurt
handful of pistachio slivers
    (or very coarsely chopped whole
    nuts), to decorate

Put the barberries into a heatproof mixing bowl, add the boiling water, and let soak for a few minutes.

Transfer the barberries and their soaking liquid to a blender and blitz to a paste.

Using an electric hand beater, whip the cream with the confectioner's sugar in a large mixing bowl. When stiff peaks form, gently fold in the barberry paste and Greek yogurt.

Serve in individual glasses, and decorate with a few extra barberries and the pistachios.

Lime & black pepper frozen yogurt

Why I didn't think of this recipe years ago is beyond me. Simply put, if you want something to refresh your palate after a heavy meal and give you just a hint of sweetness and plenty of satisfaction, then this is for you. It's probably the most surprising little sorbet you could try. It sounds like it shouldn't work but it really, really does. I love it so much I could happily eat it every day, especially when the weather is warmer.

SERVES 4

2 cups Greek yogurt
½ cup confectioner's sugar
finely grated zest and juice of 1 fat lime
1 teaspoon freshly ground
   black pepper

Put all the ingredients into a mixing bowl and stir to combine.

Pour the yogurt mixture into an ice-cream maker and churn according to the manufacturer's directions.

This frozen yogurt is best served straight from the ice-cream maker.

Roasted walnut & tahini ice cream

This ice cream is truly something else. I find myself eating it even before it's fully set. It really is at its peak as it just comes out of the ice-cream maker, when it is set but still soft and gooey enough to eat spoon after spoon.

SERVES 4 TO 6

1½ cups walnuts

1¼ cups milk

1¼ cups heavy cream

¼ cup tahini

⅓ cup superfine sugar

3 large egg yolks

Preheat the oven to 400°F.

Spread the walnuts out on a baking pan and toast in the oven for 10 to 12 minutes. Remove from the oven and let cool. Pulse the cooled walnuts briefly in a food processor (or coarsely chop) to retain some texture rather than finely grinding them, then set aside.

Heat the milk and cream gently in a saucepan over very low heat until warm. Then add the tahini and mix well until it has dissolved. Add half the sugar and stir until dissolved, then remove the pan from the heat and let cool.

Put the egg yolks and remaining sugar into a mixing bowl and whisk together using an electric hand beater until pale and thickened. Slowly pour in a little of the cooled cream mixture, stirring as you go to ensure it is quickly incorporated, then add the remaining cream mixture and mix well. Pour the entire mixture back into the pan and heat gently over very low heat. When it almost comes to a boil, remove the pan from the heat. The custard should be thick enough to coat the back of a spoon. Cool the custard (you can speed up this process by pouring it into a glass bowl and placing the bowl onto ice or into very cold water), stirring occasionally.

Once the custard is completely cold, stir in the chopped walnuts, then pour the mixture into an ice-cream maker. Churn for about 1 hour. You can serve the ice cream immediately or, if you prefer a firmer texture, transfer it to a freezerproof container and freeze for later use. If using from the freezer, let stand at room temperature for 20 minutes to soften slightly before serving.

Apple, poppy seed & lemon loaf cake

God knows I love cake. But although it is one of my great loves, I exercise a great deal of moderation and it really does have to be a very good cake in order for me to indulge. Loaf cakes are one of my favorite things to bake. They're simple and versatile and there is no tricky fiddling or sandwiching of layers. You can add frostings, vary the ingredients, and use up whatever you have without needing large quantities of anything, which is how this recipe came about. Sometimes when I buy apples and they are a bit lacking in crunch, I use them in cake rather than eat them. I prefer my cakes to be moist and fruity with lots of different flavors, and this example ticks all the boxes. Warm it up and it's great with custard or ice cream, too.

SERVES 8 TO 10

3 very small or 2 medium apples,
    quartered

3 eggs

¾ cup superfine sugar

finely grated zest of 2 lemons

1 teaspoon vanilla bean paste

½ teaspoon almond extract

1½ cups all-purpose flour

1 teaspoon baking powder

1¼ sticks unsalted butter, melted

1 heaped tablespoon poppy seeds,
    plus a little extra for sprinkling

Preheat the oven to 350°F. Line a 2lb (11 x 4½ x 2¼ inch) loaf pan with a nonstick paper liner or nonstick parchment paper.

Core the apples, keeping the skins on, and then finely dice. Set aside.

Put the eggs, sugar, lemon zest, vanilla bean paste, and almond extract into a mixing bowl and beat together until well combined. Add the flour, baking powder, and melted butter and mix again. Gently fold in the diced apple without crushing it too much and the poppy seeds.

Pour the batter into the prepared loaf pan and sprinkle the top with extra poppy seeds. Bake for 50 minutes to 1 hour (my own oven takes an hour), or until cooked through and a skewer or knife inserted into the center of the loaf comes out clean. Remove from the oven, invert the loaf out of the pan onto a wire rack, and let cool before serving.

Saffron & sesame shortbreads

I absolutely love shortbread. The buttery, crumbly goodness of it makes it the master of all cookies in my humble opinion. The saffron-tinted Persian cookies of the patisseries in my neighborhood when I was growing up provided the inspiration for this combination. But while I have enjoyed many a Persian sweet treat, they really aren't a patch on the marvelous shortbread cookie, so here it is uniquely flavored with saffron and sesame. They're perfect with sweetened black tea, which is just the way we like it.

MAKES 18 TO 20

¾ cup sesame seeds

2 cups all-purpose flour

¾ cup confectioner's sugar

generous pinch of sea salt flakes

1 ¾ sticks unsalted butter, softened

½ teaspoon saffron threads, ground
    to a powder using a mortar and
    pestle, then steeped in 1 tablespoon
    boiling water until cool

superfine sugar, for sprinkling

Preheat the oven to 425°F.

Spread the sesame seeds out on a baking pan and toast for 6 to 8 minutes until browned. Remove from the oven and let cool.

Combine the sesame seeds with the flour, confectioner's sugar, salt, and butter in a mixing bowl, then add the saffron solution and work the ingredients into a dough.

Divide the dough in half and form each half into a sausage about 1½ to 2 inches in diameter. Seal each sausage in plastic wrap and twist the ends to tightly encase the dough, like a candy wrapper. Refrigerate for 1 hour. Alternatively, freeze them and bake later.

Preheat the oven to 340°F. Line a large baking sheet with nonstick parchment paper. Unwrap each sausage of dough, then cut into slices ½ inch in thickness. Arrange them on the prepared baking pan leaving about ¾ inch of space around each one. Bake for 20 minutes. Remove from the oven and sprinkle with superfine sugar. Let cool on the cookie sheet before serving.

Pistachio, lemon & rosemary cake

The pistachio is the king of Persian nuts, and the naturally bright green color of Persian pistachio slivers helps create the electric-green shade of this cake. Fragrant with lemon zest and aromatic rosemary, it's also gluten free.

SERVES 8 TO 10

1¼ sticks unsalted butter

4 x 4-inch sprigs of rosemary, leaves picked and very finely chopped

3 eggs

⅓ cup superfine sugar

1 teaspoon vanilla extract

1 teaspoon lemon extract (alcohol-free)

2 heaped tablespoons Greek yogurt

finely grated zest of 3 large lemons

½ cup ground almonds

10½oz pistachio slivers (or whole nuts), very finely blitzed in a food processor, plus extra to decorate

FOR THE FROSTING

1¼ cups confectioner's sugar

1½ tablespoons freshly squeezed lemon juice

Preheat the oven to 350°F. Take a large square of nonstick parchment paper, crumple it up, then smooth it out and use it to line a 9-inch round cake pan.

Warm the butter in a saucepan over very low heat until just melted. Remove from the heat, stir in the chopped rosemary leaves, and let stand to infuse.

Put the eggs, superfine sugar, and vanilla and lemon extracts into a mixing bowl and beat together until well combined. Mix in the yogurt, followed by most of the lemon zest (reserve a little for decorating the cake), the ground almonds, and pistachios. Pour in the infused melted butter and mix again until evenly combined.

Pour the batter into the prepared cake pan (give the pan a shake to level off the batter). Bake for about 45 minutes until golden brown on top and springy to the touch. Remove from the oven and let cool completely in the pan.

Mix the frosting ingredients together in a small bowl until smooth.

Carefully invert the cooled cake from the pan onto a serving plate. Pour the frosting on top. Once the frosting has set, scatter with the pistachios and reserved lemon zest before serving.

Tahini, almond & orange brownies

These almond-based orange-spiked brownies are so good. Not only are they simple to make, they are even gluten free. I absolutely love combining chocolate and orange in cakes and desserts because they work so well together. But here the nuts and the wonderfully rich tahini really crank up the flavor while also keeping these little brownie squares lovely and soft.

MAKES 9 OR 12

4 eggs

¾ cup superfine sugar

1 tablespoon natural vanilla extract

finely grated zest and juice of
    2 oranges

¼ cup unsweetened cocoa powder

2 cups ground almonds

1¾ sticks salted butter, melted

¼ cup tahini of pouring consistency,
    thinned with warm water if
    necessary

3½oz dark chocolate chunks or
    ½ cup dark chocolate chips
    (70% cocoa solids)

Preheat the oven to 350°F. Line an 8-inch square cake pan with nonstick parchment paper, ensuring the paper comes up a little over the sides of the pan.

Beat the eggs, sugar, and vanilla extract together in a large mixing bowl until combined. Add the orange zest and juice and the cocoa powder and mix well. Add the ground almonds, then stir in the melted butter. Add the runny tahini and really work it well into the mixture (it will stiffen a little, so add a tablespoon of warm water if it seizes too much). Finally, fold in the chocolate.

Pour the batter into the prepared pan. Shake the pan and tap it on the work surface to settle the batter evenly. Bake for 45 to 50 minutes, or until cooked through and a skewer or knife inserted into the center comes out clean. Remove from the oven, then use the paper to lift the brownie out of the pan. Let cool on a wire rack on the parchment paper, then peel away the paper and cut into 9 or 12 squares.

TIP

These brownies are really good served with custard.

Blueberry, pistachio & coconut cake

Here's some chewy, nutty, fruity, zesty, cakey goodness with so much flavor on every level. I'm fairly sure that's all I need to tell you to get you digging out your loaf pan. If by some small miracle you are a nerd like I am and have two loaf pans, do yourself the kindness of doubling the batch and baking two cakes at once. I made friends with my new neighbors by dropping one of these off at their door. The best lesson in life I've ever learned is that you'll always win friends with cake.

SERVES 8 TO 10

3 eggs

¾ cups superfine sugar

1 teaspoon vanilla bean paste

1 teaspoon almond extract

1 teaspoon lemon extract (alcohol-free)

½ cup desiccated coconut

1½ cups unsalted butter, melted

1½ cups all-purpose flour

1 teaspoon baking powder

¼ cup milk

generous handful of pistachio nuts

1¼ cups blueberries

Preheat the oven to 340°F. Line a 2lb (11 x 4½ x 2¼ inch) loaf pan with a nonstick paper liner or nonstick parchment paper.

Put the eggs, sugar, vanilla bean paste, and almond and lemon extracts into a large mixing bowl and beat together until well combined. Add the coconut and mix well, then stir in the melted butter until incorporated. Add the flour, baking powder, and milk and mix until smooth. Finally, stir in the pistachios and then gently fold in the blueberries.

Pour the batter into the prepared loaf pan and bake for about 1 hour, or until cooked through and a skewer or knife inserted into the center comes out clean. Remove from the oven, invert the cake onto a wire rack, and let cool. Serve in slices.

White chocolate, raspberry & pistachio tiramisu

A classic tiramisu is one dessert I can rarely resist, but this recipe offers stiff competition. White chocolate and raspberries are made for each other, and the vibrant green pistachios add a nutty flourish that makes this dish the absolutely perfect way to round off a meal.

SERVES 6 TO 8

3½oz white chocolate, broken into pieces

3¼ cups raspberries

2 teaspoons confectioner's sugar

3 tablespoons cold water

2 eggs, separated

1½ cups heavy cream

9oz mascarpone cheese

¼ cup superfine sugar

6oz ladyfingers (about 18)

½ cup pistachio slivers (or whole nuts), finely blitzed in a food processor

Place the white chocolate in a heatproof bowl set over a pan of barely simmering water, without letting the base of the bowl touch the water. Let the chocolate melt, then lift the bowl out of the pan and set aside.

Put half the raspberries, the confectioner's sugar, and cold water into a food processor or blender and blitz until pureed.

Whisk the egg whites in a small bowl with an electric hand beater until they form stiff peaks. In a separate bowl, whip the cream to soft peaks.

Put the egg yolks, mascarpone, and superfine sugar into a large mixing bowl and beat together. Mix in the melted white chocolate, then add the whipped cream a little at a time, gently folding it in with a spatula to keep the mixture light. Once all the cream has been incorporated, add the whisked egg whites a little at a time, again folding them in gently rather than stirring.

Select your serving dish (I use a 10½ x 7 inch rectangular dish). Use as many ladyfingers as necessary to cover the bottom of the dish in a single layer, breaking some up if you need to fit them into corners or sides. Pour the raspberry sauce over the ladyfingers and spread it out with the back of a spoon to cover them completely, then add the whole raspberries in an even layer. Finally, pour the white chocolate mixture over the raspberry layer. Shake the dish to allow the mixture to fill any gaps, then smooth over the surface with a spatula. Scatter with an even layer of the pistachios and refrigerate for a minimum of 8 hours or overnight before serving.

Turmeric, orange & coconut rice pudding

Turmeric is an ingredient you need to be incredibly careful with when you are using it in nonsavory recipes, especially the fresh variety. If you use too much everything tends to taste like curry. This delicate pudding features the aromatic perfume of turmeric without the harsh back bite in an orange-scented coconut milk rice, making the perfect combination for a satisfyingly creamy sweet treat. Persians don't generally eat rice pudding as a dessert but as more of a snack in the afternoon or at breakfast. However you enjoy it, this is a unique recipe and definitely one to try. Just make sure you stick to the prescribed quantity of fresh turmeric!

SERVES 6

2½ cups milk, or more if needed

14 oz can coconut milk

finely grated zest and juice of
    2 oranges

¼ cup superfine sugar

⅛oz fresh turmeric, scrubbed and
    finely grated

1 teaspoon vanilla bean paste

1¾ cups short-grain rice

2 handfuls of desiccated coconut,
    plus extra to decorate

Pour the milk and coconut milk into a large saucepan and stir in the orange juice, sugar, turmeric, and vanilla. Heat gently over medium-low heat, without boiling.

Add the rice and cook for about 25 minutes until tender, stirring regularly to draw the starch out of the rice. If your rice pudding has thickened too much, simply add more milk, or cook for a few more minutes if it needs longer to soften.

When the rice is cooked, stir through the desiccated coconut and orange zest. Serve sprinkled with extra coconut to decorate.

Cheddar & za'atar rolls

I do love the combination of bread and melted cheese. It's one of life's little joys, in my humble opinion. These rolls make wonderful sandwiches as well as being a great alternative to the traditional dinner roll. Do yourself a favor and make a double batch because, if I'm honest, every time I make any sort of bread, I end up eating a hefty portion of it straight from the oven. And if you do have to share them, you may just need more than six.

MAKES 6

¼oz sachet active dry yeast

3 tablespoons milk, warmed

4 cups strong bread flour

1 cup lukewarm water

3 tablespoons olive oil, plus
    extra for rubbing

1 teaspoon sea salt flakes

3 heaped tablespoons za'atar

3½oz vegetarian Cheddar cheese, grated

Add the yeast to the warm (but not hot) milk and stir with a fork until dissolved. Then let stand for 5 minutes.

Add the flour to a mixing bowl and make a well in the center. Pour the yeast mixture into the well and use a fork to mix it into the flour as best as you can. Add the lukewarm water, olive oil, and salt, then use your hands to mix together to form a dough. Cover the bowl with plastic wrap and let rest for 10 minutes. Then knead the dough in the bowl for 1 minute. Repeat the resting and kneading process twice more.

Line your largest baking pan with nonstick parchment paper. Divide the dough into 6 balls on the lined pan, then rub with olive oil. Sprinkle each ball with 1 teaspoon za'atar and rub it all over the dough. Then sprinkle with a little more za'atar to coat evenly. Scatter an equal quantity of the cheese on top of each roll and sprinkle them with the remaining za'atar. Let rest in a warm place for 10 minutes.

Meanwhile, preheat the oven to 425°F.

Bake the rolls for 30 minutes until cooked through and the cheese turns golden. Remove from the oven and let cool before serving.

Cilantro & feta spiced loaf

You can make many wonderful breads without a bread maker. I'm not the most skilled baker by any stretch of the imagination, but this loaf is really appealing, preferably served still warm, and with a generous smear of salted butter.

MAKES 1 LOAF

1¼ cups coarsely chopped fresh cilantro

½ cup olive oil

¼oz sachet active dry yeast

3 tablespoons milk, warmed

4 cups strong bread flour, plus extra for dusting if needed

2 teaspoons coriander seeds, toasted and crushed (see Tip on page 15)

2 teaspoons cumin seeds, toasted and crushed (see Tip on page 15)

¾ cup warm water

7oz vegetarian feta cheese

sea salt flakes and freshly ground black pepper

Put the fresh cilantro, stalks and all, into a mini food processor with half the olive oil and 1 tablespoon of warm water and blitz until you have a smooth herb oil.

Add the yeast to the warm (not hot) milk and stir until dissolved. Then let stand for 5 minutes.

Tip the flour into a mixing bowl, then season generously with pepper and a good amount of salt and mix in. Make a well in the center, pour the yeast mixture into the well, and use a fork to mix it into the flour as best as you can. Add the herb oil, toasted crushed seeds, remaining olive oil and the warm water. Then use your hands to mix it all together to form a dough.

Knead the dough in the bowl for 1 minute and let rest for 10 minutes, then repeat the kneading and resting process. Knead again for 1 minute, then add large chunks of the feta to the dough, working it in by stretching the dough over the cheese to envelop it. Shape the dough into a ball (dust it with flour if it is sticky). Transfer to a sheet of nonstick parchment paper, then place in a large cast-iron dutch oven or onto a baking sheet. Cover with a clean dish cloth and let rise in a warm place for 1 hour.

Preheat the oven to 400°F.

Using a sharp knife, slice a cross in the top of the dough, then bake for 35 to 40 minutes until cooked through and browned on top (the base should sound hollow when tapped). Let cool on a wire rack before serving.

TIP
Using a cast-iron dutch oven will help to cook the loaf from the bottom.

Index

Author's acknowledgments

To my long-suffering agent Martine Carter, who has to wrangle with me constantly, but who does so with such grace and experience, and always has my best interests at heart—you know how much I appreciate and value you and there is no one better to help me do what I do. Thank you for always keeping me on the straight and narrow and caring beyond what an agent usually would; you are very much like family to me.

To my brilliant publisher and friend Stephanie Jackson at Octopus Publishing, thank you for continuing to support my ideas and working with me to create brilliant books. To the lovely Caroline Brown, Publicity Director at Octopus Publishing, and to your absolutely fantastic team who are the best in the business and work so hard on every new book; without you, Megan and Matt my books wouldn't be as well-known as they are today—you guys always knock it out of the park for me.

To my dear friend, my wonderful, brilliant photographer Kris Kirkham, you are the Zen guru of our shoots. Always funny and supportive, you get me and my food and make working with you and the entire team nothing but pure joy—thank you for yet another beautiful collection of photographs that bring my food to life on every page. And thank you to Kris's assistant, Eyder Rosso Goncalves, for his endless care and kindness on shoots, and to knowing when a recipe is extra successful because you eat it all.

An extra special thank you to my superstar editor Sybella Stephens, who has the incredibly hard task of making my recipe text make sense! Five books in and you make it look easy, but I know it's far from that.

To Jonathan Christie, Jazzy "Fizzle" Bahra, and Peter Hunt for designing and creating yet another beautiful book despite how hard it becomes each time. You have my utmost sympathy for having to work with me, but thank you for your patience and for allowing me to participate in the process.

The most unsung heroes on my photoshoots are the team who make my food look incredible and appealing on every page, so a huge thank you to my food stylist, the incredibly gifted and super-patient Laura Field, for always delivering the perfect plate of food, and to her brilliant (and also very tolerant and patient) assistants Hilary Lester, Sonali Shah, and Lizzie Evans.

I wouldn't be anywhere without the tireless efforts of the brilliant Kevin Hawkins; thank you for all your wisdom, experience and opinions that help guide what I do and have always been completely invaluable to me. A big debt of gratitude also to Alison Goff and Denise Bates at Octopus Publishing, for always being incredibly supportive and kind, and making me feel so valued. And to the entire Octopus team, those who I know and may not know, for working all the cogs that make up the bigger picture of our successes together—I am so grateful for all that you've done and continue to do for me every day.

And last, but by no means least, to my mother, Mama Ghayour… who now seems to have her own fan base across social media, who will always be blunt when critiquing my recipes and who still refuses to even try to cook, but who is the best friend, sister, father, mother, travel-partner and official PA any girl could ever ask for. You are the Thelma to my Louise and we drive each other nuts, but I wouldn't have it any other way, and despite your long list of "foods you don't like," I absolutely adore and respect you and am so grateful to have you as my Mom.